Faith It To Win!

By Ronnie Christian

Presenting Jesus
- He Still Cares -

Pen In My Hand Publishing

Faith It To Win!

Text Copyright © 2011 Ronnie Christian
www.christiancowboy.org
First Printing 2011

Pen In My Hand Publishing
P.O. Box 187, Blanco, Texas 78606
www.christiancowboy.org
For more information contact:
Christian Cowboys and Friends
P.O. Box 187, Blanco, Texas 78606
(830) 386-4936

Manufactured in the United States of America

ISBN: 978-0-9770325-2-5
Library of Congress Control Number:

- "New Testament Scriptures taken from the New American Standard Bible®, Copyright 1960, 1962, 1963, 1968, 1971, 1972, 1973, 1975, 1977, 1995, by The Lockman Foundation. Used by permission." (www.Lockman.org).
- Old Testament Scriptures are from the New King James Version unless otherwise noted. Those from the King James Version will have (KJ) after the verses.

Back Cover: Ronnie Christian winning a go-round in the Bull Riding at the P.R.C.A Rodeo in Houston.

Artwork/Ilustration by: Dale Hirschman and Tammy Zamorano
Layout and Design by: Tammy Zamorano, Kerrville, Texas

INTRODUCTION: My name is Ronnie Christian. I am a rodeo cowboy who loves Jesus and wants to bring others to know Him. I am a Lifetime Gold Card Member of the Professional Rodeo Cowboys Association.

VISION: Reach rodeo cowboys and cowgirls with the Good News that Jesus loves them and Jesus Saves. Through this, their families, friends, and the many people they contact around the world, including ranchers and others in the horse and livestock industry will know God cares for them and Jesus is Lord.

EXPECTATION: See people saved, set free, healed spiritually, physically, and emotionally, filled with the Holy Spirit, and living a life pleasing to God.

Faith It To Win!

Introduction

As you pray in faith and speak God's Word by faith, you will see amazing things happen in your life.

Faith in God pleases Him and He will move on your behalf, but when He comes with your blessings will He find faith on the earth? Will He find faith in you? If the answer is yes, expect blessings.

We see people and animals healed, pain leaves their bodies; fear goes and confidence and courage comes; rain stops or goes around rodeo arenas when we speak to it to go in Jesus Name; peace and joy are restored in people's lives. We also have favor in business deals. It is all because we place our faith in the Name above every Name, Jesus.

You can doubt and do without or you can believe and receive.

As you walk by faith you will see defeat turn to victory. You will go from sinning to winning. You will see what you are believing for come into being. We walk by faith - not by sight.

Faith in God is the winner's walk!

Matthew 9:22 "But Jesus turning and seeing her said, "Daughter, take courage; your faith has made you well." At once the woman was made well."

II Cor. 5:7 "...we walk by faith, not by sight."

Hebrews 11:1-2 "Now faith is the assurance of things hoped for, the conviction (evidence-KJ) of things not seen. (2) For by it the men of old gained approval."

Hebrews 11:6 "And without faith it is impossible to please Him, for he who comes to God must believe that He is and that He is a rewarder of those who (diligently-KJ) seek Him."

Table Of Contents

By Faith

Hebrews 11:1 "Now faith is the assurance of things hoped, the conviction (evidence - KJV) of things not seen..."

It is your **"faith in God"** that brings into being what you hope for. Hope is always in the future. Why would you hope for what you already have? But <u>your faith is now</u> - "Now faith is..." It takes faith to bring your hope into reality.

Also see Hebrews 11:6 "And without faith it is impossible to please Him, for he who comes to God must believe that He is, and that He is a rewarder of those who (diligently - KJV) seek HIm."

We must walk by faith, talk by faith, rest by faith. We never get out of the faith walk.

When you walk by faith, you have your joy even before your answer comes, because you know by faith, down "in your knower", that God is working in your situation to bring blessings to you - to meet your needs. You begin thanking God ahead of time, before you see or hear what your are believing for. It is on the way. No more worry or doubt - but instead expectancy. It's just a matter of time, but it will come - whether it is in finances,

1

healing, peace of mind, direction in life, or spiritual, physical or emotional breakthrough that is needed.

Fear and faith have something in common. They both believe something is going to happen that has not happened yet. You are going to use your time either way. So use it believing God that something good is going to happen. Do not walk in fear. *II Timothy 1:7 "For God has not given us a spirit of timidity (fear - KJV) but of power and love and discipline (sound mind - KJV)."* **Jesus talked about Great Faith; Little Faith; Unbelief - No Faith.**

GREAT FAITH - In *Mat. 8:5-13 there is a story about a Roman centurion who came to Jesus "saying, 'Lord my servant is lying paralyzed at home, suffering great pain.' (7) And Jesus said to him, 'I will come and heal him.' (vs 8) But the centurion answered and said, 'Lord, I am not worthy for You to come under My roof, but just say the word, and my servant will be healed (9) For I, too am a man under authority, with soldiers under me; and I say to this one, 'GO!' and he goes and to another, 'Come!' and he comes...' (10) Now when Jesus heard this, He marveled and said '...I have not found such great faith with anyone in Israel.' (13) And Jesus said to the centurion, 'Go your way; let it be done to you as you have believed.' And the servant was healed that very hour."*

Do you have a situation in your life that you need a breakthrough? Believe for a good report - you usually get what you believe for.

I was about to speak on the subject of faith at a Cowboy Church service after the Huntsville, Tx. PRCA Rodeo recently. I heard a bull rider tell another bull rider's wife that he had pain in his knee. He thought he had injured the ACL. By faith I laid hands on his knee and commanded his body to line up with the Word of God. I said in faith, "Everything that should be tight - be tight; everything that should be loose - be loose." Then I said, "Pain you

2

have to go in Jesus name." As I was about to walk away I told him, "Believe for a good report, you usually get what you believe for." A few minutes later his traveling partner came to the church service and told me that his friend was pain free. The now healed cowboy relayed to us how he had been skeptical when he began hearing about anointing the sick with oil and laying hands on them for healing but he smiled and said, "The pain is gone!"

LITTLE FAITH - In *Mat. 8:23-27 Jesus and his disciples were in a boat and (vs 24) "...there arose a great storm in the sea." Jesus was asleep so in verse 25 they awoke Him saying, "Save us Lord, we are perishing!" (vs 26) "And He said to them, 'Why are you so timid (fearful), <u>you men</u> of <u>little faith</u>?' Then He arose, and rebuked the winds and the sea; and it became perfectly calm."*

At a rodeo in Boerne, Tx. in 2005 the rodeo announcer in the announcer's booth said to me "Look!" Dark rain clouds were blowing straight toward us. I said, "Split and go around this rodeo arena in Jesus name." In about a minute or two we looked at each other and laughed as the clouds split and went on both sides of the arena. We enjoyed a dry rodeo It sprinkled during the last event; when the final bull was ridden and when the rodeo ended, it began to rain. God is amazing - the wind and rain still obey Him.

UNBELIEF - NO FAITH - In *Mark 6:1-6 Jesus was in His hometown. (vs 5) "And He could do no mighty miracles there except that He laid hands upon a few sick people and healed them. (6) And He wondered at their unbelief."* No faith here - there were no mighty miracles.

Remember - *"God has given every man a measure of faith." (Romans 12:3)* Use it and it will grow. Always trust God.

Jesus went to the cross by faith. What He did had never been done before. He died for my sins and yours by faith. By faith He knew He would live again. And because He lives we can live forever with Him. But we must believe in Him and receive Him by faith. We are saved through faith.

Ephes. 2:8 "For <u>by grace</u> you have been <u>saved through faith</u>; and that not of yourselves, it is the gift of God; (9) not as a result of works, so that no one may boast."

BY FAITH CALL ON JESUS TO SAVE YOU: Jesus is the only way to heaven. *John 14:6 "I (Jesus) am the way, and the truth, and the life; no one comes to the Father, but through Me."* Receive Jesus now by faith. Pray, "Dear God I am a sinner. Forgive my sins. I receive Jesus as my Savior and Lord. I turn from sin to You and Your way of living. By faith I call to You and know I am now saved, eternal life is mine, Heaven is my home. Baptize me, fill me with the Holy Spirit for power to be a bold witness for You. In Jesus Name - Amen." (Now read Rom. 3:10, 3:23, 5:8, 10:8, 9-10, 13, John 3:16, Luke 3:16, Luke 11:13 Acts 2:38, Acts 1:8)

2   **It Is Well**

II Kings 4:26 "...Is it well with you? Is it well with your husband? Is it well with the child? And she answered, 'It is well.'" This was spoken just after her son had died.

     This is a great story of faith about the Shunammite woman whose son was raised from the dead (found in II Kings 4:8-37). In verse 16 Elisha prophesied that the Shunammite woman who had no children would have a son in about a year. She did give birth to a son but as he was working in the field with his father, his head ached so they took the boy to his mother where he died in her lap. She decided to go to the man of God. In verse 23 she said, "It is well" (or at this time it could mean "It will be well"). As she approached Elisha, his servant asked her, "Is it well with you?...your husband?...the child? And she answered, 'It is well.'" She went from "It will be well" to "It is well." This is a great statement of faith and she tells Elisha (in verse 30), "And the mother of the child said, 'As the Lord lives, and as your soul lives, I will not leave you.' So he arose and followed her." <u>She made a demand on Elisha's faith.</u> The result of her faith came in verse 34-37 - <u>the boy came to life</u>.

     Can you say, "It is well?"

     Learn to say, "It is well?"

     Are you sick? It is well. Jesus is the healer. Have you lost your job? It is well. God is your provider and will give you a better one. *Phil. 4:19 "And my God shall supply all your needs according to his riches in glory in Christ Jesus."* Are you at the end of your rope? It is well. That is where God hangs out. *Ps. 107:27-30 "They reel to and fro, and stagger like a drunken man, and are* at their wits' end. *(28) Then they cry out to the Lord in their trouble, and He brings them out of their distresses, (29) He calms the storm, so that its waves are still. (30) Then they are glad because they are quiet; so He guides them to their desired haven."* Has the enemy beaten you up? It is well. II Thes. 3:3 *"But the Lord will strengthen you and protect you from the evil one."* Psalm 25:15 *"My eyes are ever toward the Lord, For He shall pluck my feet out of the net. "*

In Exodus 14 when the Egyptian army came after Moses and the children of Israel, it looked very bad, but God was watching and knowing - "It is well." The Red Sea departed, Moses and the people passed through on dry land and the Egyptians were drowned.

Time after time God delivered His people. He will deliver us too. *Hebrews 13:8 tells us "Jesus Christ is the same yesterday and today, yes and forever."*

Notice He delivered His people. The Lord knows those who are His.

When Jesus was in the grave, it looked bad to His disciples, but with God, "It is well." On the third day, God raised Him up to live again. He took the sting out of death for us. "It is well." He will raise us up also to live forever.

John 6:63 "It is the Spirit who gives life; the flesh profits nothing; the words that I have spoken to you are spirit and are life."

Learn to fight the good fight of faith - don't lose heart, consider your trials as momentary light affliction; walk by faith not by sight (II Cor. 4:16-18 and II Cor. 5:7).

How about you? Is it well with you for eternity? If your eternal destiny is not settled, do it now. Jesus will give you eternal life. Pray this to receive His gift. "Dear God, I am a sinner. I need a Savior. Forgive me and cleanse me from my sins. I accept what

Jesus did for me on the cross when He shed His Blood on the cross to wash my sin away. I turn away from sin and turn to You and receive Jesus into my life right now as my Savior and Lord. Thank you for dying for me and preparing a place for me forever in heaven. Holy Spirit, help me live a life pleasing to my Father in heaven. I can now say, "It is well with my soul! I am Saved!" Read Romans 3:10, 3:23, 5:8-9, 6:23, 10:9-13, John 3:16, Acts 2:38.

It Is Well!!

Romans 8:9-11 "However, you are not in the flesh but in the Spirit, if indeed the Spirit of God dwells in you But if anyone does not have the Spirit of Christ, he does not belong to Him. (10) If Christ is in you, though the body is dead because of sin, yet the spirit is alive because of righteousness. (11) But if the Spirit of Him who raised Jesus from the dead dwells in you, He who raised Christ Jesus from the dead will also give life to your mortal bodies through His Spirit who dwells in you

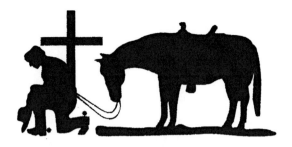

Be Specific
When You Ask

Matthew 7:7 "Ask and it shall be given to you; seek and you shall find; knock and it shall be opened to you. (8) For everyone who asks receives, and he who seeks finds, and to him who knocks it shall be opened. (9) Or what man is there among you, when his son shall ask him for a loaf, will give him a stone? (10) Or if he shall ask for a fish, he will not give him a snake, will he? (11) If you then, being evil, know how to give good gifts to your children, how much more shall your Father who is in heaven give what is good to those who ask Him!"

Elijah prayed and it did not rain for three years and six months in Israel, then he prayed again and it did rain. What did Elijah pray for? - RAIN. Specifically, they needed rain. That is exactly what he asked for and that is what the people received. The story is in I Kings chapters 17 and 18. First off, the people of Israel had turned from God. He had declared earlier that if they turned from Him and served other gods that He would withhold rain from their land. Israel had a wicked King named Ahab who along with the people had turned to worship the false god, Baal. In a contest between Elijah and the prophets of Baal, they prepared two bulls, one for the prophets of Baal to offer up to Baal and one for Elijah to offer up to the one true "God who answers by fire."

The prophets of Baal cried out to their false god for hours but nothing happened. Then Elijah called for fire from heaven and God answered by fire and consumed the sacrifice, the wood, the stones, the dust and the water that Elijah had told the people to pour on and around the bull. Elijah asked specifically for fire and that is what he got. *I Kings 18:39 "Now when all the people saw it, they fell on their faces, and they said, 'The Lord, He is God! The Lord, He is God!'"* They turned back to God and this put them in a position to receive blessings again. Specifically they needed rain. In verse 40 Elijah executed all 450 prophets of Baal. In vs. 41 Elijah says by faith "...there is the sound of abundance of rain." In vs. 42 Elijah gets in a posture of prayer. In vs. 43 He sent his servant to go look for rain - the servant saw nothing and Elijah said seven times "Go again." He had asked God for rain and he kept looking for his answer. In vs. 44 the servant said, "...There is a cloud as small as a man's hand..." So Elijah, although there was very, very little evidence of rain told King Ahab, "Prepare your chariot and go down before the rain stops you." And in verse 45 "...there was a heavy rain."

Things to learn from this story

(**1.**) Elijah prayed specifically for rain. We need to pray specifically. Do you need a job? Pray specifically for the job or type of job you need and want. Do you need help? Pray specifically for what kind of help you need. (**2.**) The people had turned from God and stopped the flow of blessings and instead received a curse. (**3.**) When the people turned back to God it put them in a position to receive the blessings of God again. (**4.**) Elijah was specific, and also persistent. He sent his servant back seven times to look for the rain he had prayed for. (**5.**) The initial report of a cloud was that it is a very small cloud. He began praying in faith and stood in faith even when the evidence was nothing at first. End result was an abundance of rain (**6.**) Elijah received the answer through effective fervent prayer. (**7.**) We can do the same as reported in James 5:16-18 (16) "Therefore confess your sins to one another, and pray for one another, so that you may be healed. The effective [fervent [KJV]) prayer of a righteous man can accomplish much. (17) Elijah was a man with a nature like ours, and he prayed earnestly that it might not rain; and it did not rain on the earth for three years and six months. (18) And he prayed again, and the sky poured rain, and the earth produced its fruit."

BE SPECIFIC IN YOUR PRAYERS

The story of two blind men is recorded in Matthew 20:24-34. Two blind men heard that Jesus was passing by and cried out, saying, "Lord have mercy on us, Son of David." The multitude told them to be quiet "but they cried out all the more, saying, 'Lord, have mercy on us, Son of David.'" Vs. 32 "And Jesus stopped and called them and said, 'What do you want me to do for you?'" Obviously He knew, but God wants us to verbalize our requests to Him in a very specific way. Vs. 33 "They said to Him, 'Lord, we want our eyes to be opened.' Vs. 34 says "And moved with compassion, Jesus touched their eyes and immediately they regained their sight and followed Him."

Things to learn from this story

(1.) They cried out to the Lord more than once, even when others said, "Be quiet." **(2.)** He knew their need yet He wanted them to specifically ask for what they wanted. **(3.)** They got specific. **(4.)** They received their sight.

Another story in Matthew 8:5-13 - The Roman centurion asked Jesus to only say the word and his servant would be healed. Jesus, seeing his faith, healed his servant that very hour.

Thing to learn -

Ask in faith. Remember God is not moved by needs; **He is moved by faith.**

In Matthew 8:1-3 In verse 2, a leper came to Jesus and said, "Lord, if you are willing, You can make me clean." (vs3) "And He stretched our His hand and touched him, saying, 'I am willing, be cleansed.' And immediately his leprosy was cleansed."

Things to learn

(**1.**) The leper was very specific in his asking. Be specific. (**2.**) Jesus is willing to answer prayer.

Also in Matthew 15:29-31, the multitudes came. What do you think they came for? The blind came to see, the deaf came to hear, the dumb came to speak, the lame came to walk, the crippled came to be restored and that is exactly what they got.

A cowboy came to a cowboy preacher, one year about 1980-1982 at the Ft. Smith, Arkansas rodeo and asked him to pray and agree with him for a new roping saddle. He was asked,, "What kind?" The cowboy responded, "A Howard Council roping saddle." He said, "Show me one." They walked around and found one on a horse. They prayed the prayer of agreement. This was in May. In July a few weeks before the big rodeo in Cheyenne, WY the cowboy received not only one but two Howard Council roping saddles. He received one by bus in a box, not even knowing where it came from. Get specific, ask with the right motives, keep your heart right with God, ask in faith, stand in faith, trust in God, receive your answer, give God the glory when it comes.

Have you specifically asked Jesus to forgive your sins ands to come into your life and to be your Savior?

Rev. 3:20 "Behold I stand at the door and knock; if anyone hears My voice and opens the door, I will come in to him, and will dine with him, and he with Me." He will come in if you ask. Pray this, "God I am a sinner, I need a Savior, I ask you to forgive me of all my sins. I ask Jesus to come into my life and be my Savior and the Lord of my life; I ask for eternal life with You in heaven. I thank You that right now I am saved. Heaven is my home. I ask You Holy Spirit, to help me live a life pleasing to my Father in heaven. In Jesus name, Amen. *Read Romans 3:10, 3:23, 5:8-9, 6:23, 10:9-10, John 3:16, Acts 2:38.*

chapter

4   Belief And Action

Acts 8:12 "But when they believed Philip preaching the good news about the Kingdom of God and the name of Jesus Christ, they were being baptized, men and women alike."

Actions should follow what we believe as Christians, disciples and followers of Jesus Christ.

The group of people that heard the message Philip preached acted on their belief by following the Lord's instruction to be baptized. They did this in obedience. They did this as a witness to others. This signified that the old man had died and now they were rising up out of the baptismal waters to walk in newness of life. (See Romans 6:4)

As you gain insight of Bible truths actions should follow.

I believe - therefore I pray. (Action)

John 15:7 (Jesus said) "If you abide in Me, and My words abide in you, ask whatever you wish, and it shall be done for you."

Spend time in God's word; let it become a part of you. Spend quality time in prayer and you will begin to take on the nature of Jesus. You will become as He is. Your prayers will line up with what God wants for you which is always the best. You will begin to see more and more answered prayers and blessings. Take time to pray.

I believe I'm forgiven - therefore I forgive. (Action)

I John 1:9 says in part - "If we confess our sins, He is faithful and righteous to forgive us our sins..." The moment you sincerely ask for forgiveness and repent, or turn away from that sin, and are willing to change, God cleanses you by the blood of Jesus

12

and you become righteous in His eyes. He totally forgives and even forgets your sins. He wants us to be like Him in our treatment of others. Therefore, we must forgive. *Matthew 6:14-15 "For if you forgive men for their transgressions, your heavenly Father will also forgive you (15) But if you do not forgive men, then your Father will not forgive your transgressions."* Unforgiveness leads to bitterness which will eat you up like a cancer. Bitterness leads to rebellion. Rebellion leads to hate. Forgive and you go back to love.

If you don't feel like forgiving someone - choose by an act of your will to forgive them - your feelings will catch up later. Unforgiveness will block the blessings of God in your life. No one and nothing is worth messing up your relationship with the Father.

I believe God heals - therefore I pray for the sick. (Action)

Mark 16:17-18 says in part (17) And these signs will accompany those who have believed... (18) ...they will lay hands on the sick and they will recover." Jesus laid hands on the sick - they were healed. He told his disciples to heal the sick - they did and the sick were healed. We should pray for the sick, lay hands on the sick and speak to sicknessess and fevers as Jesus did. We are to be moved with compassion as Jesus was and is - and the same Jesus who is the same yesterday, today, yes and forever (Hebrews 13:8) will heal today.

We believe the Word - We preach the Word. (Action)

II Corinthians 4:13 "But having the same spirit, according to what is written, I BELIEVED, THEREFORE I SPOKE, We also believe, therefore also we speak."

We believe the Word of God, we speak the Word of God and God confirms His Word by signs following. (see Mark 16:20 below).

When God's Word is spoken and received lives will change. Hatred turns to love. Confusion is exchanged for wisdom. The sick are healed. Drug addicts and alcoholics are set free. Families are restored. The lost get saved. Meanness turns to kindness. God gives you beauty for ashes and joy for mourning. Peace comes as we believe and act on the Word of God. When we preach the Word something should happen - something will happen. *Mark 16:20 "And they went out and preached every-where, while the Lord worked with them, and confirmed the Word by signs that followed."* (Action).

Acts 16:31 And they said, "Believe in the Lord Jesus, and you shall be saved, you and your household."

Delayed
But Not Denied

Galatians 6:7-10 "Do not be deceived, God is not mocked; for whatever a man sows, this he will also reap. (8) For the one who sows to his own flesh will from the flesh reap corruption, but the one who sows to the Spirit will from the Spirit reap eternal life. (9) Let us not lose heart in doing good, for in due time we will reap if we do not grow weary. (10) So then, while we have opportunity, let us do good to all people, and especially to those who are of the household of the faith."

Even when we are doing what is right in God's eyes, things sometimes do not go well and it seems like - "it's just not working."

But know this - God is faithful to His word and promises. Jeremiah 1:11 declares He watches over His Word to perform it. And II Tim. 2:13 says even if we are unfaithful, He remains faithful.

Don't grow weary in doing good. Keep planting good seeds of love, joy, peace. Do what is right and good and true like King Hezekiah (II Chron. 31:20-21). Every work he did, he did it with all heart for God and he prospered. Do the same and you will prosper too.

Remember whatever you sow you will reap. (See Gal. 6:7 above). If you don't like your crop (what is happening in your life) - sow better seed. If you are sowing good seed, keep watering it with prayer, with the word of God, and a good confession, speaking life over yourself and others. Do not love in word and tongue only but in deed and truth (II John 3:18). Your blessing is coming.

Reaping and sowing takes time. Give and it shall be given

(Luke 6:38) is a process. It's like my beans, corn and potato message.

When you plant beans they come up in just a few days. Corn takes a little longer, but then you see a stalk. You can peep inside and see there is corn growing. Potatoes are a faith crop all the way. They grow underground. When you sow into this or other ministries and churches, your seed is planted; expect it to grow. Your harvest - (blessing) may come to you quick, a little slower or even very slow but when it is time, your harvest (blessing) will burst on the scene suddenly.

Heb. 10:35 "Therefore, do not throw away your confidence, which has a great reward."

Matthew 24:13 is talking about eternity with Jesus. "But he who endures to the end shall be saved." Don't be denied heaven. Jesus' blood paid for you to be there (I Cor. 6:20 and Heb. 10:19).

A few years back, I was in our CCF office looking at our financial report. I said, "People say, 'That's great what you are doing.'" But I looked up and said to God, "It ain't working." Then I drove to an old country church which has a Texas Historical Marker on the outside wall; it is used now for special occasions. It was unlocked so I went in. I walked up to the pulpit of the empty church and preached to myself. I quoted as I read *Is. 61:1-3 "The Spirit of the Lord GOD is upon Me, because the LORD has anointed Me to preach good tidings to the poor; He has sent Me to heal the brokenhearted, to proclaim liberty to the captives, and the opening of the prison to those who are bound; (2) to proclaim the acceptable year of the LORD, and the day of vengeance of our God; to comfort all who mourn, (3) to console those who mourn in Zion, to give them beauty for ashes, the oil of joy for mourning, the garment of praise for the spirit of heaviness; that they may be called trees of righteousness, the planting of the LORD, that He may be glorified."*

I walked out the door. A week or two later I did the same thing and I prayed over every pew (bench seat) as I walked out the door. Then I was off to fulfill my purpose and ministry. I was delayed, but not denied. I am still preaching in the good and the bad times.

Sometimes we need others, we need to go to church, we need friends - but at times we need to encourage ourselves in the Lord like King David did at Ziklag (I Sam 30). He sought the heart and mind of God. Then David went on to pursue the enemy and got back everything and more that the enemy had stolen.

Jacob (Gen. 29) worked seven years for Rachel, but her father gave her sister, Leah,to him. So he worked another seven years for Rachel. He was delayed in getting Rachel at first, but he was not denied.

Joseph kept his heart right when he was sold by his brothers into slavery. He became the head of his master's (Potiphar's) house. When falsely accused by Potiphar's wife, Joseph went to jail. But when he interpreted the King's dream, Joseph was made the second highest in position and power in Egypt. (See Psalm 103:17-21) He was delayed, but not denied.

The whole army of Israel was delayed by the challenger, Goliath, the giant. David, as a young boy, took his sling shot and hit the giant in the head with a rock. When Goliath fell over, David took the giant's own sword and cut off Goliath's head. Then Israel attacked and won the battle. Again delayed, but not denied.

Paul, the apostle, was going to Rome. On the way he and the crew of the ship had a ship wreck. He was delayed, but not denied. Paul got to Rome (see Acts 27 and 28:14).

Perhaps your breakthrough in finances is delayed; your healing is delayed; your marriage problems are causing the life of love and success to be delayed. Don't limit God! Do not be denied. Stay faithful to God - do not be delayed any longer - be blessed - do not be denied!

Don't be denied getting your heart right with God. Don't be delayed in getting forgiveness of sin, receiving Jesus as Savior and Lord. Do this and receive eternal life and make heaven your home.

I John 1:9 "If we confess our sins, He is faithful and righteous to forgive us our sins and to cleanse us from all unrighteousness."

Romans 10:13 "for whoever will call on the name of the Lord will be saved."

Don't delay - Receive Jesus - Receive Eternal Life.

Don't Sell Your
Birthright

6

(You Are A Member Of The Church
Of The Firstborn)

Your Inheritance   Joy Land $$$ Health

Houses   Eternal Life   Abundance

Peace Of Mind   Livestock

*Hebrews 12:6 "that there be no immoral or godless person
like Esau who sold his own birthright for a single meal."*

Esau, being the oldest, had a birthright to inherit the most.
He made light of it and did not consider it's value properly. He
sold his birthright to his brother, Jacob, for a single meal. We have
a birthright because we are in the body of Christ. We have bless-
ings to receive, so we need to examine ourselves to see if we have
made light of our birthright as children of God and sold our
birthright for some passing pleasure of sin, through disobedience,
through not guarding our hearts and minds or through not letting
God have first place in our lives.

Hebrews 12:15 *"See to it that no one comes short of the
grace of God; that no root of bitterness springing up causes trou-
ble, and by it many be defiled; (16) that there be no immoral of
godless person like Esau, who sold his own birthright for a single
meal. (17) For you know that even afterwards, when he desired to
inherit the blessings, he was rejected, for he found no place for
repentance, though he sought for it with tears."*

Here is the story. It's in Genesis 25:29-34. In verses 29-30- *Esau came in hungry. Jacob had cooked some stew. Esau asked for some to eat.* (vs 31) *"But Jacob said, 'Sell me your birthright as of this day.'"* (In vs 32) *Esau said that he was about to die so* (in vs 33) *he sold his birthright to Jacob for a meal, then* (in vs 34) *Esau ate and drank but then he despised his birthright.*

Esau was the oldest. As such, in the custom of Haran where they lived, the oldest son would inherit headship of the family and a double share in the inheritance, but a man could sell his birthright. Esau's desire for the present and tangible at any cost left him without his birthright. Because he chose immediate passing fleshly gratification, the blessings that were to be his were lost forever. Let this be a lesson to us. Even when we are forgiven some of our choices have consequences that can not be reversed. God will take all things and work them for our good. Some things will be restored, others will not. But God will restore our peace and joy even with some things being lost forever. At times God makes it better than it was before the loss when we get our heart right with God again.

Now in Genesis 27 the boys' father, Isaac, decided to bless his son, Esau, before he died. But Jacob tricked his father whose eyesight was now bad and his mom, Rebekah, helped in the deception. It was her idea to begin with. So Isaac blessed Jacob instead of Esau. When Esau arrived **it was too late.** He had sold his brother his birthright and now be missed the blessings of the oldest son.

Let's see what birthright we have and why. Jesus is sometimes referred to as the firstborn from the dead. Col. 1:15 *"He (Jesus) is of the invisible God, the first-born of all creation. (16) For by Him all things were created, both in the heavens and on earth... (17) And He is before all things and in Him all things hold together. (18) He is also the head of the body, the church; and He is the* beginning, the first-born from the dead; so that He Himself might come to have first place in everything."

When you receive Jesus, you are born again; **you are in the church of the firstborn.**

In Hebrews 12:22 *But you have come to Mount Zion and to the city of the living God, the heavenly Jerusalem, and to myriads of angels. (23) to the general assembly and **church of the firstborn** who are enrolled in heaven, and to God, the Judge of all, and to the spirits of righteous men made perfect. (24) and to Jesus, the mediator of a new covenant, ..."*

All of us receive an inheritance when we receive Jesus Christ. In Christ it is not just the eldest or first who are born again - it's for all of us! Our inheritance is love, joy, peace, eternal life, good health, prosperity, soundness in spirit, soul and body and clear direction plus many more good things.

III John 2 *"Beloved I pray above all things that you prosper and be in good health just as your soul prospers."*

So don't sell your birthright. What is keeping you from your birthright of blessings? One lady doctor was overweight for 45 years because she said she would always eat one more meal. She felt like she had sold her birthright for a meal. But God in His mercy restored it when she repented. Now she looks and feels better and is in better health and better condition. Her action was to change her eating habits. She did what she could in the natural and God handled the super natural.

What areas have you sold your birthright? Is it sex, tobacco, alcohol, anger, overspending, bad attitude, unforgiveness, bitterness, anorexia, bulimia, ungodly music and movies, laziness, blatant sin, wrong relationships, wasting time - the list goes on. Find out what is holding you back from the good things in life and root it out of your life; take authority over it in Jesus Name. Walk free from it and see the blessings from your birthright become real in your life.

Do You Have The Believer's Birthright? Are you in the church of the first-born? The Bible says in John 3:4 that Jesus said, *"...unless one is born again, he cannot see the kingdom of God."* and John 3:7 *"...You must be born again."* To be born again is to be born from above, born of God not of man. Being born again gives you eternal life and a home in heaven. If you want this pray - "God, I am a sinner, I need a Savior. I ask you to forgive me of my sins, come into my heart and my life. I accept what Jesus did on the cross when he died for me and His blood washed away my sin. I believe He arose again. I believe He is the Son of God. I accept Jesus now as Savior and Lord. I now have a birthright to receive eternal life and blessings on this earth. I am now in the church of the first-born. Holy Spirit help me live a life pleasing to my Father in Heaven. In Jesus name I pray, Amen. Now get baptized, confess Jesus is your Lord to others, read the Bible and pray everyday and you will learn more about your birthright with blessings that are yours; meet often with other believers in church and elsewhere. Read Roman 3:10, 3:23, 5:8-9, 6:23 and John 3:16 and Acts 2:38.

Our birthright is to be filled with the Holy Spirit. - Ask Jesus to baptize you in the Holy Spirit for power to be bold in your life in Jesus Christ. Luke 11:13, Acts 1:8; 4:29-31.

chapter

7

Go Back
To Your First Love

***Revelation 2:3 (Jesus said) "and you have perseverance and
have endured for My name's sake, and have not grown
weary (4) But I have this against you, that you have left your
first love."***

Every person and every church in every age can be found in
Revelation chapters 2 and 3. These are letters written to seven
churches from Jesus as prophesied and revealed through His angel
to John the apostle. Read these chapters to see where you are in
your relationship with God - you will see yourself and your
church.

There is no other place Jesus should occupy in our lives but in
first place - He is to be our first love. The moment you received
Jesus, He became your first love. Your eyes were on Jesus, the
author and perfector (finisher - KJV) of your faith (Heb 12:2).

When you first fell in love with Jesus you knew you were
loved, forgiven of all sin, accepted, pure, clean. You did what was
right in God's eyes because it was right, not because of rules and
regulations. When you were in your first love you knew the Holy
Spirit was living big in you. You listened to His voice, and were
quick to obey. You gladly did what He said because you knew you
could trust Him with your future.

When you were in your first love you were quick to forgive;
you did not take offense easily. When you were in your first love
you knew you could trust God; you knew He would answer your
prayers; you knew He was working things out for your good.
When you were in your first love you spoke the word of God with
confidence and boldness and authority. When you were in your

23

first love, fear had no grip on you. *I John 4:18 "There is no fear in love; but perfect love casts out all fear..."* Yes, when you walked in your first love things were different. You were not tempted to sin as easily because sin did not interest you. When you were in your first love you sought out the good in others and gladly served others. When you were in your first love you were eager to share how good Jesus is and how much people need Him. You loved people as Jesus does. You were not so quick to judge people but rather showed the love of God. You showed forgiveness. You told people about eternal life they could have through Jesus Christ our Lord.

When you were in your first love, your light for God was shining. See *Matthew 5:16 "Let your light shine before men in such a way that they may see your good works and glorify the Father who is in heaven."* When you were in your first love you knew God is a good God who does good things for people.

Ps. 31:15 "My times are in Your hand..." Your future is secure in Jesus. *Acts 10:38 "You know of Jesus of Nazareth, how God anointed Him with the Holy Spirit and with power, and how He went about doing good and healing all who were oppressed by the devil, for God was with Him. "*

When you were in your first love you served the Lord and you served others with gladness. You had confident expectation and hope for the best in every day life.

When you were in your first love you were quick to repent when you did sin. You changed directions, quickly confessed your sin and got back on the path of Jesus without hesitation.

When you were in your first love the fruit of the Spirit could be seen in your life. *Gal. 5:22-23 "But the fruit of the Spirit is love, joy, peace, patience, kindness, goodness, faithfulness, (23) gentleness, self-control; against such things there is no law."*

If you have left your first love, Jesus tells us what to do.

Repent! Change directions - get back to a close walk with God. *"Draw near to God and He will draw near to you..."* (James 4:8)

If you do not repent Rev. 2 says He "will remove your lamp-stand out of its place unless you repent." Your light won't be shining for God even if you still do religious things like go to church and read your Bible. Your church may exist, but the light won't be shining..

He tells us to listen to what the Spirit says to the church.

He wants us to repent for our good. His desire is for us to eat of the tree of life in the Paradise of God - to be with Him forever enjoying His presence.

Just think - we will eat of the tree of life that Adam could have eaten in the Garden of Eden. It is the tree of life eternal. That is the desire Jesus has for us. Read Rev. 2:1-7.

In Rev. 3:7-13 the Church in Philadelphia is mentioned. Jesus will keep you from the hour of testing which will come upon the whole earth; so go to your first love, Jesus, and you can be in this church. That is the church I claim I belong to. But in Rev. 3:14-22 the Church of Laodicea is a lukewarm church that Jesus will spit (vomit) out of His mouth. Even then He instructs people to repent because He cares for them. He knocks at their door. When they open He will come in and grant that they sit down beside Him on His throne in Heaven.

Make sure Jesus is your first love. The tree of life and a place with God forever awaits you.

Question: What are you allowing in your life now in words or actions that you did not allow when you were in your first love with Jesus? If there is something, repent. He will gladly forgive you and cleanse you by His blood.

Make Jesus Your First Love: Dear God I ask you to forgive me of my sins. Jesus you loved me first before I loved you. Thank You for dying on the cross for me and taking away my sin. Thank you for giving me eternal life. I receive you now as my Savior, my Lord

- you are now my first love. I desire to live for you. Holy Spirit guide me all the days of my life. In Jesus Name. Amen. Romans 3:10, 3:23, 5:8-9, 6:23, 10:9-10, 13, John 3:16, Luke 11:13, Acts 1:8, Acts 2:38, Rev. 22:14.

chapter 8
God Is Not Just Taking Us Through Something - He Is Taking Us To Something!

Psalm 18:29 For by You (God) I can run through a troop; and by my God I can leap over a wall.

God takes us through battles, storms, and troubles, then to peace, victory, love and calm. Jesus went through the battle of the cross to victory over death. And now He brings us to eternal life.

Psalm 23:4 "Yea though I walk through the valley of the shadow of death, I will fear no evil; for You (God) are with me. "

It looks like death sometimes but it is only a shadow, not the real. We've been through shadows before - we're still here!

It may seem like death of your finances, death of your business or career, death of a dream, death of a relationship or death of your good health. God is your Defender, your Guide, your Supplier, and your Deliverer. Remember *Lamentations 3:21-26 "His mercy is new every morning."* Keep your hope in God. You will come out a better person and in better shape. *Mat. 28:20 (Jesus said) "and lo I am with you always, even to the end of the age."* (and the end of your battles).

Moses took about 3 million Hebrews through the Red Sea - not over or around but through. They had been in the desert for days. Now Pharaoh's army was coming after them, but God opened the Red Sea and took them to safety. Pharaoh's army - the enemy - drowned as the Sea covered them. God will cover our enemies and cause us to see them no more. *Isaiah 41:12 "You*

27

shall seek them and not find them... Those who war against you shall be as nothing, as a non existent thing."

Next Moses and the people walked around in that desert for 40 years as God took them through their bad attitudes until they were ready, and then He took them to the Promised Land.

In the battle, the Holy Spirit will teach us. We will learn from each battle and come out better as we listen to Him and do what He says. To win our battles requires: (1) Being teachable (2) trusting God (by faith) (3) being patient (4) using wisdom from God's word (5) being obedient (Is. 1:18-19) (6) being humble (James 4:10) (7) Repenting where necessary (8) keeping our love walk pure with God and others.

When we learn and get in line with God's will - we are on our way to victory!

If you have known sin - confess it, get forgiven of it, learn from it, then go on (John 1:9). It is not God but it is sin withholding good from you. *Jer. 5:25 "...and your sins have withheld good from you."*

Pride will get you in and keep you in a battle until you humble yourself and turn back to God. Daniel 4:28-37 Nebuchadnezzar boasted of his kingdom and his accomplishments. He took the glory - he gave no glory to God. He was then driven out to eat grass like the animals for seven years until he lifted his eyes up to heaven. He gave glory to God and was restored as the King again.

Quit trying to get through in your own strength. Keep your eyes on Jesus, the author and perfector (finisher) of our faith (Heb. 12:2). Jesus is the path to victory. His name is above all names and all battles. (see Phil. 2:9-11)

Jesus Takes You To Heaven: Jesus is the only way to heaven. John 14:6 "Jesus said to him, 'I am the way, and the truth, and the life; no one comes to the Father, but through Me.'" Pray: Dear

God forgive my sins. Thank you for sending Jesus to die for me on the cross. I receive Jesus right now as my Savior and the Lord of my life. Thank you that I am now a child of God. You will take me through everything in life to take me to heaven. Holy Spirit help me to live a life pleasing to my Father in heaven. In Jesus Name I pray. Amen. Now get water baptized, ask Jesus to baptize (fill) you with the Holy Spirit, read the Bible and pray everyday. Read Romans 3:10, 3:23, 5:8-9, 6:23, 10:9-10 & 13; John 3:16; Acts 1:8; Acts 2:38.

chapter
9

He Kept Giving -
Let's Keep Giving

In Mark 6, the story is told of the multitudes coming to Jesus in a desolate place. As it began to get late, the disciples told Jesus that He should send them away so they could go and buy something to eat in the villages. ***Mark 6:37-44 (37) "But He answered and said to them, "You give them something to eat!" 38) And they said to Him, "Shall we go and spend two hundred denarii on bread and give them something to eat?" 39) And He commanded them all to recline by groups on the green grass. 40) And they reclined in companies of hundreds and of fifties. 41) And He took the five loaves and the two fish, and looking up toward heaven, He blessed the food and broke the loaves and He kept giving them to the disciples to set before them; and He divided up the two fish among them all. 42) And they all ate and were satisfied. 43) And they picked up twelve full baskets of the broken pieces, and also of the fish. 44) And there were five thousand men who ate the loaves."***

Look again at verse 41 - He took; say, "He took." He blessed; say, "He blessed." He broke; say, "He broke" and He kept giving; say, "He kept giving." The result was He fed 5,000 men plus women and children and there was an abundance left over.

I was reading the Bible recently wanting to read about Jesus praying. I came across Mark 6 about the multiplication of the fish and loaves. Jesus blessed, prayed over the meal. Jesus is our prime example of what to be like.

I was in my morning prayer and Bible time and reached over and got my checkbook. I said, "same deal as the fish, Lord. There is not enough here to meet every need of the ministry right now. So, I am taking this checkbook. I lift it up to you and I bless it to you. I am going to write a check to the youth ministry I had vowed to support. So, I am <u>breaking</u> it and I will keep <u>giving</u>." I wrote the check, gave it to another minister in town to deliver to the youth minister.

I shared that story about five days later at "Cowboy Church - Bandera", which we held on Monday nights. Those who were giving that night <u>took</u> their tithes and offerings, <u>blessed</u> it to the Lord, <u>broke</u> apart the portion they would give and <u>gave</u>. When it was counted, about 14-15 times more than the normal offering came in - this was less than a week after this ministry gave the above mentioned vow or pledge money to the youth ministry.

Something similar happened that week again - an extra amount came in through our financial partners in the mail. Of course, the financial seeds we plant don't always return that soon. The next week we kept giving without seeing an immediate return but we are determined to be like Jesus and keep giving.

Galatians 6:9 "And let us not lose heart in doing good, for in due time (season) we shall reap if we do not grow weary."

Be a giver. Give of yourself. Give love, time, money, talent, prayers, service. Keep giving - the Bible declares that in blessing you shall be blessed.

God is a giver. He gave us His Son to die for our sins so that we could be forgiven and go to Heaven to live eternally with Him.

Jesus is a giver. He gave His life - a ransom for you and me and got us out of the grip of Satan and sin and hell.

The Holy Spirit is a giver. He gives us life. Just as He raised Jesus from the dead, He will also give life to our mortal bodies. He gives direction, convicts us of sin, reveals Jesus to us, helps us pray, leads, guides, teaches, gives us spiritual gifts to equip us to be better Christians and to help others. He gives us strength to overcome temptations and boldness to be a witness to others about Jesus. He gives us love, joy and peace.

Yes God is truly a giver - let's be givers.

Look at the Lord's supper (communion). He took the bread, He blessed it, He broke it, He gave it.

Look at Jesus Himself - He let the soldiers take Him, His Father blessed Him, He was broken, and He gave Himself to and for us.

What does God do with us? He takes us in whatever condition He finds us, He blesses us so we can become what He wants us to be and we can fulfill the purpose He has for us here. He breaks us of sinful attitude, so we can be of good service to others. He gives us to a lost, dying and hurting world to show them the love of God and give them hope and victory here and now and in the age to come, eternal life.

Jesus came to give. He did His job very well. God was pleased with Him and said, *"This is My beloved Son, in whom I am well pleased." Matthew 3:17.*

Let's also give our lives to God and others and one day God will say to us, "Well done, good and faithful slave (servant); you were faithful with a few things, I will put you in charge of many things, enter into the joy of your Master." (Matthew 25:21)

Jesus was given as a gift to you - receive Him - receive the gift of eternal life and joy today.

Pray: I receive You, Jesus, right now as my Savior and Lord of my life. Forgive me, the sinner, of all my sins. Take me, bless me, break me, give me to others to show Your love for them. God is now my Father; heaven is now my home. Thank you Lord - in Jesus Name. Amen. Now read Romans 3:10; 3:23, 5:8-9; 6:23; 10:9-10, 13, John 1:12-13; John 3:16; Luke 11:13; Acts 1:8; Acts 2:38.

Give Your Life: Let's determine to give our lives to Jesus and to others in an increasing way.

chapter

10

Hot, Cold or Lukewarm

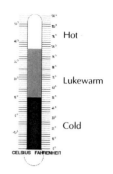

Hot

Lukewarm

Cold

CELSIUS FAHRENHEIT

Revelation 3:15 "I know your deeds, that you are neither cold nor hot; I would that you were cold or hot (16) So because you are lukewarm, and neither hot nor cold, I will spit you out of my mouth."

God is looking for a people to bless not curse. He knows your deeds. As He sees, He judges; it is either punishment or rewards.

II Chron. 16:9 "For the eyes of the Lord run to and fro throughout the whole earth, to show Himself strong on behalf of those whose heart is loyal to Him. In this you have done foolishly; therefore from now on you shall have wars." God was watching King Asa of Judah. Asa did what was right. God helped him win wars although he was greatly outnumbered. Then Asa made a treaty with the ungodly King of Syria to fight together against Israel instead of relying on God. God came to bless him but what He saw brought the curse of continual wars to Asa and all Judah instead. Asa became diseased in his feet, but in this he did not seek the Lord but physicians, and he died. He started out doing good - he was hot for God - then he cooled down and had a tragic end. Jesus taught in *Matthew 24:13 "He who endures to the end shall be saved."*

God desires sincerity. He desires our heart. He desires us to be hot for God, zealous for good deeds, serving Jesus and loving others.

33

The cold ones are easy to spot. They don't care about the things of God. He loves them - they don't love Him back.

The lukewarm bunch are the ones described in *Titus 1:16* *"They profess to know God, but by their deeds they deny Him, being detestable, and disobedient, and worthless for any good deed."* They will come to (cowboy) church service, pray before they ride (in the rodeo or compete in other areas) - then they go out and party with the world.

James 4:4 "You adulteress, do you not know that friendship with the world is hostility toward God? Therefore whoever wishes to be a friend of the world makes himself an enemy of God."

A lukewarm person is someone who says, "I believe in Jesus" but does not live like it. He may even say, "Jesus is Lord", but really, he is his own lord - his flesh rules his life. The desires for other things choke the word of God out of his life. *Mat. 6:33* says *"Seek first the kingdom of God and His righteousness; and all these things shall be added to you."*

A lukewarm person cannot keep his peace. He has moments of being close to God - but runs back into sin. He feels bad because the Holy Spirit is convicting him of the wrong he does. Then when he tries to do right, the devil condemns him and says he is not worthy of being a child of God.

To the lukewarm I say, "Turn up the heat!
Get hot for God!"

What the hot ones do. They put God first (Mat 6:33). They hunger and thirst for righteousness. (Mat. 5:6) They walk in love, stand up for what is right, easily forgive, exhibit the fruit of the Spirit (Gal. 5:22-23 - love, joy, peace...), confess Jesus before men, Jesus is their Lord - the Boss, Master. They are zealous for good deeds, hate sin and hate evil. They are led by the Holy Spirit.

The cold ones. They run swiftly to evil, do not care about the things of God, sin often, not willing to repent (change), reject Jesus as Savior. Their flesh rules.

I Cor. 6:9-11 "Or do you not know that the unrighteous shall nor inherit the kingdom of God? Do not be deceived; neither fornicators, nor idolaters, nor adulterers, nor effeminate, nor homosexuals, (10) nor thieves, nor the covetous, nor drunkards, nor revilers, nor swindlers, shall inherit the kingdom of God. (11) And such were some of you; but you were washed, but you were sanctified, but you were justified in the name of the Lord Jesus Christ, and the Spirit of our God." Verse 19 states to those who received Jesus that "your body is a temple of the Holy Spirit." Verse 20 goes on "For you have been bought with a price; therefore glorify God in your body."

Make a commitment to honor Jesus with your life. After Jesus talked about being hot, cold or lukewarm in *Rev. 3:15-16* above He finishes by saying in verse 19 *"As many as I love, I rebuke and chasten (discipline). Therefore be zealous (eager) and repent." (20) "Behold I stand at the door and knock. If anyone hears My voice and opens the door; I will come in to him and dine with him, and he with Me." (21) "To him who overcomes I will grant to sit with Me on My throne, as I also overcame and sat down with My Father on His throne." (22) He who has an ear, let him hear what the Spirit says to the churches."*

Get hot for God. *Romans 10:13 "Whoever calls on the name of the Lord shall be saved."* Pray. Oh God, I am not right with you; I am cold, I need a Savior. Forgive my sins. I call on Jesus right now to be my Savior, and Lord. Thank You for dying on the cross and shedding Your blood and giving Your life to save me. I confess, 'Jesus, You are my Lord.' I turn from being cold to hot for God. Holy Spirit I will do what you show me to do; help me to please God with my life. In Jesus Name I pray. (The lukewarm can pray the above prayer inserting lukewarm for cold). Now read Rom. 3:10, 3:23, 5:8-9, 6:23, 10:9-10, 13, John 3:16, Acts 1:8, 2:38. See Luke 6:46-49; James 1:22.

11

In This Place!

Isaiah 46:9-10 "Remember the former things of old, for I am God and there is no other. I am God, and there is none like Me (10) Declaring the end from the beginning..."

Remember the good things God has done.

I was at the P.R.C.A. Rodeo in Jacksonville, Texas again in July to minister and hold Cowboy Church services. I've been doing this annually for over 10 years. The Rodeo Committee is very friendly and open to us having church as are rodeo producers' Scotty and Tonya Lovelace of Classic Pro Rodeo. When Jesus is welcome it sets the atmosphere for blessings.

I was getting ready to preach one night this year and I began to "remember the former things of old" that God had done in this place at this rodeo arena.

II Peter 1:13 "And I consider it right as long as I am in this earthly dwelling, to stir you up by way of reminder."

I remember what Jesus has done in this place at the Jacksonville Rodeo grounds.

1) Last year - 2008 - A bull rider was healed of knee injury during Cowboy Church service. A barrel racer was healed of shoulder and elbow pain - in this place!

2) The night before - 2008 - A bareback rider led a bull rider to pray to receive Jesus and changed his eternal destiny. Now, that same bull rider was here tonight at Cowboy Church to learn more about his walk with Christ Jesus.

I John 5:11-13 "And the testimony is this, that God has given us eternal life, and this life is in His Son. (12) He who has the Son has the life; he who does not have the Son of God does not have the life. (13)These things I have written to you who believe in the name of the Son of God, so that you may know that you have eternal life."

3) Six years ago - At another arena. The mother of a bare-back riding student at a rodeo school in Fredericksburg, Texas, was healed of M.S. (Multiple Sclerosis). Several years later in this place she watches the rodeo every year. She confirmed to me how God had healed her.

4) A few years ago - I held a small Cowboy Church one night after the rodeo behind the bucking chutes. A young contestant received Jesus and came to Cowboy Church in the grand stands the next night to begin to "grow in the grace and knowledge of our Lord and Savior Jesus Christ" (II Peter 3:18)

5) 3-4 years ago - A young bull rider had his collar bone come out of joint. I told two other new Cowboy Church pastors who were from a town nearby to anoint him with oil and pray. That is what James 5:14-15 tells us to do. I said, "You need to get used to doing this stuff." The next week the bull rider told me he gave a testimony at his home church about how God healed him and he was riding bulls again. It happened <u>in this place!</u>

6) 1981 - I tore a groin muscle as I was stretching getting to ride in the Bareback Riding event. I tried to ride that night plus the next night also in Brownwood, Texas. The pain was too much. I ate healing Scriptures for a week and by faith drove 1,000 miles from Texas to Wyoming to ride the next week. Eight days after I tore my groin muscle, I as winning the first-go round at the Daddy of 'Em All Rodeo in Cheyenne, Wy. with no pain in my leg. I went to a rodeo in Colorado that night and made a winning ride-again with no pain. What seemed like a <u>battle in this place</u> that would keep me out of competition for a few months was the start of a victory story.

7) Last night 2009 - A phone call came to me from a cowboy preacher in Wyoming. He went through a divorce and was wounded. But he received peace and healing of a wounded spirit - over the phone in this place.

8) Last night 2009 - Two teenage girls were healed of a wounded spirit at Cowboy Church. I don't think they knew we were having a service. Immediately as they walked near to us, Jesus began to minister to their hurts and heal their past pains.

9) 2-4 years ago - A girl that attends every year with her husband was healed of a knee injury at Cowboy Church in the grand stands. On the way home another pain hit her and she took what she learned and spoke healing to her body in Jesus' Name. She was instantly healed - twice in one night.

10) Over the years - People over the years have received Jesus as Savior and Lord of their life. People have asked Jesus to baptize them in the Holy Spirit and fire! People get peace. It's been great to see God move in people and save, heal and set the captives free <u>in this place!</u>

This is all great for the people who have been blessed by God in this place. **But God is not limited to one place. Make your place a place of blessings!** Welcome Jesus! Welcome the Holy Spirit! Receive the blessings of God. **Wherever you are you can say, "God change my life - in this place!"** (wherever you are).

In this place called heaven - God will receive you into His special place called the family of God in heaven and give you eternal life. We all will leave earth one day - will you go to heaven? You can! Romans 10:13 "Whoever calls on the name of the Lord shall be saved." Pray this - "I call on You today, Lord Jesus, to save me, to forgive my sins, to wash me clean by the blood you shed on the cross. I receive You today as my Savior and my Lord. Baptize me in the Holy Spirit and fire so I can serve you with power and bring others to know You. Thank You for giving me a place in Heaven. In Jesus name.

Read: Romans 3:10; 3:23; 5:8-9; 6:23; 10:9-10, 13; John 3:16; Acts 1:8; Acts 2:38; Mark 16:15-20.

chapter

12

Intimate With God

James 4:8 "Draw near to God and He will draw near to you..."

As I was about to prepare for Cowboy Church at the PRCA Rodeo in Jacksonville, Texas I began to pray silently in the Spirit (in tongues) and God began speaking to me. He gave me the message for the Cowboy Church service that night - and I feel it should be shared with others.

This is what came to me:

"I desire a close relationship with you. I want to be intimate with you. It's time to lay down any weights, wrong attitudes and behaviors, all encumbrances, all sin, presumptuous sin, secret sin, hidden sin, all wrong thinking that is keeping us from being close; I desire companionship, I desire friendship; lay down your hurts and let me heal your heart; lay down <u>anything</u> that keeps or puts a wall between us. I have told you in My Word - "Draw near to Me and I will draw near to you. You spend much time fighting the devil - Draw near to Me - I will get in the fight with you - then your battle plans will change and your battles will change. With Me you will win. You will come out in better shape and will be a better person. Be intimate with Me: learn to trust Me and trust Me again. I will give you strength for the journey and you will have rest for your soul. Stay close to Me and My ways and you will enjoy the trip called life much much more. I give you love, joy, peace. I give My presence. I give You My Son afresh. My Son was intimate with Me when He walked on the earth. He spent much time in prayer. We had good visits when He pulled away to be alone with Me. Do likewise. Pull down the walls and distractions and the desire for other things that block our relationship. Draw near to Me. I am ready to walk, run, sail and fly through life with you. It will be exciting. Get ready for the ride. It will be a good one."

See Heb. 12:1-3; Mark 4:18-19.
- Moses went up to talk to God on the mountain.
- Moses, Aaron, 2 sons, 70 elders had wine and bread in God's presence.
- Jesus touched people, ate in their homes, cooked the disciples fish.
- Jesus gives abundant life.

Moses went up to talk to God on the mountain several times. (See the book of Exodus). Moses, Aaron with his two sons and 70 elders of Israel went up to meet God and drank wine and ate bread in His Presence. Jesus touched people, ate in their homes, cooked the disciples fish after He arose from the grave. Jesus is Lord! Be intimate with Him. *He says, "I have called you friend..."* (John 15:15)

Jesus is intimate with the Father - He wants us to be also, so He died for our sins to reconcile us to God, to give us eternal life and to give us abundant life here on earth. He wants to walk through life with us and spend eternity with us.

To be intimate with God, receive Jesus as your Savior and Lord, be led by the Holy Spirit who comes to live in you and spend time reading the Word (the Bible) and in prayer - talking and listening.

Are You Intimate With God: Rev. 3:20 (Jesus said) "Behold I stand at the door and knock; if anyone hears My voice and opens the door, I will come in to him; and will dine with him, and he with Me." For eternal life and intimacy with God, pray this and mean it in your heart." Dear God I am far from you. I am a sinner. I desire to be close to you. Forgive my sins. I receive Jesus as My Savior and Lord. I receive what He did for me on the cross to bring me to You and grant me eternal life. Jesus is my Lord. God is now my Father. Stay close to me. I desire to be intimate with you as your child. In Jesus Name, Amen.

Now read Romans 3:10, 3:23, 5:8-9, 6:23, 10:9-10, 13, John 3:16, Acts 1:8, 2:38.

Joy In The Trials

chapter

13

From Trials To Faith To Patience
To Victory To Strength

James 1:2-4 Consider it all joy, my brethren, when you encounter various trials, (3) knowing that the testing of faith produces endurance. (4) and let endurance have its perfect result, that you may be perfect and complete, lacking in nothing."

Look what happens when we face various trials. The Bible says we are to "count it all joy." A trial is the time for testing of your faith. Then the testing of your faith produces patience or endurance. Patience or endurance has a work so in the end we are "lacking in nothing."

When the battle is over we are stronger. Then what happens? Another trial and we go again - the testing of faith, patience (or endurance), then we lack nothing. The battle is over and we are stronger, stronger.

But then what comes again? Right - another battle. So here we go again the testing of our faith, patience, we win and are lacking in nothing. Then we are stronger, stronger, stronger.

Now we are strong in the Lord, strong in our faith, our confidence and trust in God is increased. We have experience with battles. Then another trial comes to us and what happens - JOY!! Why ? Because we know with God all things are possible and we are "more than conquerors through Him who loved us" (Romans 8:37) The joy of the Lord is our strength! He brought us through before. He will bring us through again.

We are strong now and we will go into this next trial with joy walking by faith with our confidence in God. We rely on the Holy Spirit to guide us in the battle, knowing God is Jehovah-rohi, our Shepherd. We will keep our joy in the testing of our faith which will once again produce patience (or endurance) which has it's perfect work until we are complete, lacking in nothing.

So, if you are in a trial, know God's plan is for you to be "complete, lacking in nothing." Don't stop until you get the victory.

The middle of a testimony is never a good place to stop.
Never stop in the middle of your testimony.

We have read Bible stories and heard the wonderful testimonies of people who have had great victories. We have heard of financial miracles, health restored, lives being cleaned up and put on the right track, people being saved from what seemed like certain death. Remember, to have these great victories, they had to have great battles. No battle - No victory. No test - No testimony. God brought them through. The key word is "through." He brought Moses and the Hebrews "through" the desert. He did not take them around or over, but through. God says, "...I will never leave you nor forsake you." (Hebrews 13:5) Don't leave Him; don't stop trusting God in your battle. I know we all seem to lose a few fights but in Christ we will never lose the war.

My son, Caleb, was in intensive care the first three weeks of his life. If we would have stopped in the middle of the testimony, he would be dead. My faith was definitely tested. But God was faithful. Caleb came home when he was 30 days old. That was in 1989 and today he is now healthy and strong.

Whatever trial you may get into, ask God for wisdom to go through it.

James 1:5 "But if any of you lacks wisdom, let him ask of God, who gives to all men, generously and without reproach (without finding fault), and it will be given to him."

Ask in faith. God will give you a plan, a course of action. That course may be to pursue or it may be to wait. Do whatever He leads you to do. Go in His wisdom. Then you can go in joy knowing in the end you will be complete, lacking in nothing.

Let's see the cycle one more time - (1) the trial (2) testing of your faith (3) patience or endurance (4) lacking in nothing - victory! (5) you will be stronger. Then you have joy over the victory, yes, enough joy to last, if and when you go into another trial. You consider this new trial a joy knowing God will bring you through.

Jesus went to the cross and died for us, He went through His ultimate trial and won the victory over death for Himself and for all who receive Him as Savior and Lord. He did not stop in the middle of His testimony. He rose again. Those of us who have received Him can live in victory in this life and we too will overcome death and live eternally with Him.

Jesus did not stop in the middle of His testimony. Do not stop in the middle of yours.

Simply put - trust God in your battle, and He will bring you through the battle as a winner in life.

chapter 14 Keep Your Peace! Keep Your Joy!

During a troublesome time in my life, as I was taking a shower, Jesus began speaking to me about peace and joy. He said, "Ronnie, this is a definite. I died for your peace. I hung on the cross for your peace. Keep your peace. All hell may be breaking loose against you. People may reject you. People may come against you, but keep your peace. I died for you to have it. You can lose it, but don't, I hung on the cross and shed My blood for your peace. The first thing I told the boys (His disciples) when I came out of the grave was, 'Peace be with you.' I am the Prince of Peace. Keep your peace. So I said, "I receive peace."

"And another thing, keep your joy. This is a definite. I hung on the cross and died for you to have joy. It's a fruit of the Spirit - love, joy, peace... So keep your joy. All hell may be coming against you, people may reject you, people may come against you, but keep your joy. I died for you to have joy - so keep your joy. If you don't have joy, choose joy." So I said, "I choose joy."

"But I did not die to keep you out of trouble; as a matter of fact if you stay down there (on earth) long enough you will have lots of it. But, I will be with you in all of it. (Editor's Note: See John 16:33)

Now, here is why you can keep your peace and joy in the middle of the mess. Isaiah 46:10 says, 'I declare the end form the beginning' and Ecclesiastes 7:8 says, 'The end of a thing is better than the beginning.' That's why you can keep your peace and joy - because I declare a good end for you. You may not like the battle or the time, it takes - but, keep your peace and your joy and look to the end. Keep your eyes on the good ending." (This is not a direct quote but close).

Remember, God is the Master at taking something bad and making it good. *Romans 8:28 "And we know that God causes all things to work together for good to those who love God, to those who are called according to His purpose."*

So again I say, "Keep your peace and keep your joy! Receive it from Jesus."

Everyday, people are in church hearing and/or saying or reading these words "Peace be with you!" They come in with no peace and they leave with no peace. They forget to say "I receive it." God is not the author of confusion, the devil is. Jesus is still speaking these words to us, "Peace be with you!" Say this, "I receive it" Now ask for joy to replace the heaviness, the worry, the doubt, the hurt, or the war within you. Say, "I receive joy in the place of heaviness and hurt." If you have a wounded spirit, tell God; He will be happy to fix it. Say it out loud "Lord I've been hurt and I have a wounded spirit. I am asking you to heal it Lord. In Jesus name."

Expect to laugh and smile again soon. *"...for the joy of the Lord is your strength." (Nehemiah 8:10)*

DO YOU KNOW THE PRINCE OF PEACE? You can know the Prince of Peace, Jesus, personally. He will come into your life, into your heart if you ask HIm to. If you want the peace and joy of God and know you need a Savior pray this, "Dear God I am a sinner, I need a Savior. Forgive my sins, I receive Jesus Christ as my Savior and Lord. Thank you Jesus for dying on the cross for me to have eternal life and also peace and joy from you in this life on earth. Thank you for giving me a home in Heaven. Jesus is now my Lord! In Jesus name, Amen." Read Romans 3:10, 3:23, 5:8-9, 6:23 and John 3:16 and 3:36. Now get baptized, read the Bible everyday, pray everyday, meet with other believers in Christ regularly.

chapter
15

Kingdom Laws
For Success

Matthew 16:19 (Jesus said to Peter) "I will give you the keys of the kingdom of heaven; and whatever you shall bind on earth shall be bound in heaven, and whatever you loose on earth shall be loosed in heaven."

Matthew 6:33 "Seek first the Kingdom of God and His righteousness; and all these things shall be added to you ."

The kingdom of heaven is in heaven. The Kingdom of God is here in the earth as well. The Kingdom of God is "His way of doing things," So Mat. 6:33 is saying to us "seek first <u>God's way of doing things</u> " and His righteousness, then all the things you need will be provided.

Different states have different laws and different countries have different laws. The Kingdom of God has laws and principles to live by that are different than man's laws.

God has given us Kingdom Laws and Kingdom Principles. Seek them out, learn them, do them by faith and see the results God blesses you with.

THE LAWS OF THE KINGDOM

(1) The Law Of Love - *1 Cor. 13:8 "Love never fails." 1 Peter 4:8 "Love covers a multitude of sin."*

(2) The Law Of Reciprocity - *Luke 6:38 "Give and it shall be given to you..." Genesis 12:3 In blessing you shall be blessed; in cursing you shall be cursed.* Give smiles - get smiles. Give money - get money. Give people time - people will give you their time.

(3) The Law of Responsibility - *Luke 12:48 "...And from everyone who has been given much, much will be required; and to whom*

47

they entrusted much, of him they will ask all the more" We have responsibility to use our gifts, talents, time, money and position to serve God and to serve others. We have the gospel and we have to get the gospel to the world.

(4) The Law of Use - See *Matthew 25:14-30 In this parable the master said to his slave, in verse 21, that he had done well and that "you were faithful with a few things, I will put you in charge of many things, enter into the joy of your master."* When you are faithful with a little, God will allow you more and you will be faithful with much. *Verse 29 "For to everyone who has, more shall be given, and he will have an abundance; but from the one who does not have, even what he does have shall be taken away."* Use your talents or lose them!

(5) The Law of Seed Time and Harvest Time - *Genesis 8:22 "While the earth remains, seed time and harvest, cold and heat, winter and summer, and day and night shall not cease."* What you plant will come up. We are constantly planting seeds, whether good or bad seeds, and we are constantly reaping from those seeds we have sown. Sow good seeds of love, time, money, help into others. Give God something to work with and see the blessings of God spring up in your life.

(6) The Law of Sowing and Reaping - *II Corinthians 9:6-11 Verse 6 "Now this I say, he who sows sparingly shall reap sparingly; and he who sows bountifully shall reap bountifully. (10) Now He who supplies seed to the sower and bread for food, will supply and multiply your seed for sowing and increase the harvest of your righteousness; (11) you will be enriched in everything for all liberality..."* God loves a cheerful giver (verse 7). So you never donate, you never just give - you always sow. Find good ground, a good ministry producing good fruit, and sow liberally, and not only will others lives be enriched, but God will enrich your life as well, in joy, health, peace, love, money, good relationships and any area of need you have.

(7) The Law of Diligence - Our work habits and lifestyle affect us greatly. God blesses us with health, our minds, our education, giftings, and talents. He gives - now we must use them to the fullest. *Proverbs 10:4 "He who has a slack hand becomes poor, but the hand of the diligent makes rich." Prov. 12:24 "The hand of the diligent will rule, but the lazy man will be put to forced labor."* Don't say, "I'll just work hard then and not be a tither and a giver." You will miss the blessing of the giver. Don't say, "I'll just give and wait on God to return it back in multiplied form." You will miss the blessing of the diligent worker. Do both, work hard, be a giver and enjoy the blessings of both.

(8) The Law of First Fruits - *Ezekiel 44:30 "The best (or first) of all first fruits of any kind, and every sacrifice of any kind from all your sacrifices, shall be the priest's; also you shall give the priest of your ground meal, to cause a blessing to rest on your house."* When you give to God <u>the first of your increase</u> you are saying to Him, "there is none above you Lord. You hold 1st place in my life." You see it's not about money - it's about lordship; it's about putting God first. When you give to God first, it takes the curse off and puts the blessing on all that remains; it will go further than the whole 100% would have gone. God gave his first born Son and took the curse off all mankind and put the blessing on those who receive Him.

(9) The Law of the Spirit of Life - versus - The Law of Sin and Death - *Romans 8;1-2 "There is therefore now no condemnation for those who are in Christ Jesus, who walk after the Spirit and not after the flesh (vs 2) For the law of the Spirit of life in Christ Jesus has set you free from the law of sin and death."* The Old Testament Law of Moses pointed the sin out to the people. The New Testament law of the Spirit <u>points us to the grace of Jesus</u>, who takes away the sin of the world. Follow after Jesus - He is life eternal.

(10) The Law of Freedom - *John 8:31-32, 36 Vs 31 "...If you abide in My word, then you are truly disciples of Mine; (32) and you shall know the truth and the truth shall make you free." (36) If therefore the Son shall make you free, you shall be free indeed."* Jesus will make you free from sin and the penalty of sin, which is death. Instead, He will give you abundant life. He will set you free from anything that is holding you in bondage - a bad attitude, drugs, alcohol, anger, overeating, bitterness, sexual sins, debt, and any other thing that is keeping you from enjoying God's best.

(11) The Law of Eternal Life - There is no law of eternal life; <u>it is a gift</u>! *Ephes. 2:8 "For by grace you have been saved through faith; and that not of yourselves , it is the gift of God; (9) not as a result of works, that no one should boast."*

You see, we are not talking about the Old Testament law, we are talking about Kingdom laws and Kingdom principles with which to live for the blessings of God.

Jesus operated in the Kingdom of God laws. Jesus was a busy man. He was about His Father's business. He was a giver- but He also was a worker. He worked all the way to the cross to give us <u>the one thing we could not work for - eternal life</u>!

Have you received? You don't have to work your way to Heaven, you can't. However you can receive what Jesus did for you, you can receive Him. Pray this - "I am a sinner I need a Savior. I receive what Jesus did on the cross for me when he died and washed my sins away by His blood. I receive You, Jesus, into my heart and life to be my Savior and the Lord, the Boss of my life. I receive eternal life right now. Heaven is now my Home, God is now my Father. Help me Holy Spirit to live a life pleasing to You. In Jesus Name, Amen.

Lord, How Does The Kingdom Of God Work?

(A message from God)

I asked this question of my Father in Heaven. **"Lord, How Does The Kingdom Of God Work?"** He impressed upon me the following: "There are Kingdom Laws - principles that My Kingdom functions with.

<u>First</u> the foundation of the kingdom of God must be established. The foundation holds it all together. **The foundation is love.** I love all My creatures - I love the world - I created it. <u>As I love you, you must love Me</u> in return for the kingdom of God to work for your benefit. Remember *Mark 12:29-30 Jesus answered 'The foremost is Hear, O Israel! The Lord your God is One; (30) and you shall love the Lord your God with all your heart and with all your soul, and with all your mind, and with all your strength.'*

Next, My Kingdom works as I designed it when you have **love for one another**. For the people on earth to enjoy a life of peace and blessings and have joy they must love one another <u>in deed and in truth.</u>

As you build on the foundation, you must add other things. Remember, the motivation is love and love will produce other actions and fruit for the kingdom. You will bring others in to My kingdom and My family.

Love produces giving. **Be a giver.** When you give you are planting (sowing) seed. When you give you will receive back with increase from God and from man. It is a kingdom law - the law of reciprocity. Give and it shall be given. There is seed time and harvest time. Remember Gen. 12:3; Luke 6:38; Gal. 6:7-9 This law works in the natural and the spiritual.

My kingdom also <u>works in your behalf when you are faithful</u> to use what I give you. This is the **law of use.** When you are faithful in a little I will entrust you with more.

As I increase you and your goods, you have more responsibility. It is the **law of responsibility.** When a person squanders his talent and possessions and duties he loses them. When a person is diligent in his business he prospers and succeeds. So, **diligence in your work,** will cause the kingdom of God to function best.

Seeking first God's kingdom and His righteousness will cause your needs to be met. Remember, Matthew 6:25-34. Matt. 6:33 'But seek first the kingdom of God and His righteousness and all these things shall be added to you.'
Understand that first belongs to Me - it is the **Law of First Things.** I call it first because there is more to come when you honor Me first. When you give the first of your increase to Me I will put a blessing on the rest. When you give first to My kingdom it tells me where your heart is and Who has first place in your life. See Proverbs 3:9-10.

Also you must get **wisdom** - it is the principle thing. When you get wisdom you will get **understanding** and **instruction** and **knowledge.**

You will get these by spending time reading My Word and praying - talking and listening to Me.

The kingdom of God works when things in your life are in <u>proper order.</u>

The kingdom of God <u>works by authority</u>. You must understand My authority and also your authority. You must submit to the authority placed over you. I have all authority and I give you authority! Exercise your authority over the devil, sickness, disease, fear, evil, discouragement and every perverse thing and enemy of your spirit, soul and body. You have authority through My Son Jesus Christ over all the power of the enemy. See Luke 10:17-19.

The kingdom of God works when you speak **with authority. Speak blessing!** When you speak My words through My Son's Name, by the power of the Holy Spirit, no force can overtake and overcome you. Your problems will go. Your mountains will move. Pain, sickness, any spirit of heaviness and confusion will go. Death itself will flee as you speak life. My Son spoke life and He spoke it with authority while He walked the earth - you can do the same. 'As He is so also you will be in this world.' See I John 4:17.

Speak blessings - your circumstances will change for the good.

Know this - the blessing is stronger than the curse. Sin brought a curse on the earth and into peoples' live. My Son Jesus died for you - He took the curse - He became a curse for you - He restores you to Me - He even abolished the sting of death. Receiving My Son Jesus Christ gives you victory over death! He gives you eternal life! He gives you abundant life! Eternal life in My kingdom comes by repenting, turning from sin to Me, and accepting what My Son Jesus did before and on the cross and also after the cross. He rose again from the dead so you too can rise again also.

My kingdom works by My Spirit. I am the Holy Spirit. I am the One who raised Jesus from the dead and will also raise My children from the dead. I give life!

My kingdom functions on behalf of My people when they listen to Me and do what I say. Listen and be **led by the Holy Spirit.** Learn My voice. I will lead you and guide you into all truth. I will show you how to live and what to do.

There is **power in My kingdom by the Holy Ghost.** My Son Jesus will baptize My people in the Holy Spirit - this is for those who want the Spirit without measure, those who want to walk in the authority I desire for them.

You must learn to **trust Me** in My kingdom.

And you will do the above by faith. **Walk by faith** and you will see the kingdom of God promises come into being. **Faith pleases Me.** Faith says you believe Me - you trust Me. When you see and believe and speak by faith - you will then see it in the natural.

Remember never lose your hope. **There is hope in My kingdom.** I place hope in you. I declare the end from the beginning. The end of a thing is better than the beginning. In My kingdom, I place **My glory** on you. And it is 'Christ in you - the hope of glory!'

Continue in My love, in faith, in Me and in the hope I give. Keep pressing in to become like My Son Jesus. Keep reading My Word. Keep praying. I will reveal more to you as you stay close to Me. I will show you how the kingdom works. I am in control in My kingdom. You are safe and your future is secure. I have put eternity in your heart. All is well in the kingdom of God."

Living in God's Kingdom now and for eternity: You can become a kingdom son or daughter right now. Pray - Dear God, I am a sinner. I ask You to forgive me. I accept your Son Jesus Christ as my Savior, my Lord, my Master, my Best Friend, my King of Kings. Thank you Jesus for dying for me on the cross and taking my sins on yourself. I believe your Blood washed my sins away. I am now a child of God; help me to live in a pleasing way to you in the earth - in the kingdom of God. Thank you for giving me eternity to live with you in Your Kingdom in Heaven. In Jesus Name I pray, Amen

chapter
17 **Make The Trade**

I Peter 5:6 "Humble yourselves, therefore, under the mighty hand of God, that He may exalt you at the proper time (7) casting all your cares on Him because He cares for you."

Now Jesus said in *Matthew 11:28-30 "Come to Me, all who are weary and heavy-laden, and I will give you rest (29) Take My yoke upon you, and learn from Me, for I am gentle and humble in heart; and you shall find rest for your souls (3) For My yoke is easy, and My load is light."*

As I minister across the country, I find people who are worried and anxious about many things. There are many around us everyday with broken hearts, wounded spirits and in fear and worries about their finances, business, job security, children, marriage, health, abilities, education, and future. Their question is, "Will I make it?" Can I get through this? Can God fix this? Will God fix this? Am I going under? What can I do? And the under lying thought is from the spirit of fear saying, "You're not going to make it through this one. This will never change. There is no victory for you."

But that is not what Jesus says. He says I have come to destroy the works of the devil. I have come to save you. I have come to give you peace of mind and rest for your soul. Your soul is your mind, your will and your emotions.

The devil wants us to live in fear, inferiority, doubt, unbelief, anxiety and depression.

Jesus gives us courage, confidence, faith, peace, rest and lifts up our head and gives us joy.

What is the solution? What can we do? I tell people **"MAKE THE TRADE."**

Trade your cares for His rest. I have seen this work for many people and watched them smile again and have the peace of God and rest and confidence restored.

Do this. Close your hand. Inside that fist in the palm of your hand is all your troubles. Now do what God says to do - What does He say? - *"Cast all your cares on Me."* So now open your hand and give them to Him - extend your hand toward Him. While your hand is still open, as you give your cares to Him, leave it open to receive. Say, "I am giving this to you Lord - it is too heavy for me. But You said Your load is light. You said, *'Take My yoke upon you. My burden is light and you shall find rest for your soul.'* I need Your rest, so I am trading my heavy load for your light load. I put my faith in You now. I release my problems to your care. I know I can trust You." If it helps take a deep breath and say "I receive Your peace and rest and joy once again. I know I can trust You."

I have seen many people do this and get immediate relief from the oppression that the devil, situations, and other people bring. Hope is restored. God wants us to rest in Him, to trust Him.

If you do this and tomorrow or next week or sometime later you look down at your hand with a closed fist and realize you took it back. Say "I'm sorry God, I took it back." And trade Him again. Sometimes it only takes once but if it takes a few times, keep trading, because one of these times you will not take it back. You will leave it with God forever and He will totally restore you.

When we go to God and say, "I can not do this on my own, I need Your help," that shows us to be humble. And when we are humble then God will exalt us. (See 1 Peter 5:6 above).

The Bible is full of stories of people who came to Jesus one way and left better than before. They brought their troubles to Him and left them with Him. Parents brought their children with demons whom He cast out. The blind called out to Him and He gave them sight. The crippled came to Jesus and left walking. The woman who was about to lose her two sons to a debtor, came to Elijah, and God miraculously gave her enough to pay her debts, and more to live on. The woman who was looked down on, who was known to all to be a sinner came and washed Jesus feet with her tears. She was restored, her sins forgiven and she was saved. (Luke 7:36-50) Mary Magdalene had seven demons cast out. She was set free and became a well known follower of Jesus Christ. She was accepted and so are you. She was there at the tomb after He arose from the dead. She was the first to go tell the good news - "He is alive."

And of course there were thousands upon thousands in the Bible stories and in today's world who are worried about death, about eternity. What will happen if I die? How do I know I will be in Heaven? How do I know I will have eternal life.

Cast your cares upon Him because He will surely gives you rest now and for eternity.

Jesus said in *John 14:1-7 "Let not your heart be troubled; believe in God, believe also in Me. (2) In My Father's house are many dwelling places; if it were not so I would have told you; for I go to prepare a place for you." (vs 6) "Jesus said, 'I am the way, and the truth and the life; no one comes to the Father but through Me. (7) If you had known Me, you would have known the Father also; from now on you know Him and have seen Him.'"* Jesus also said in *John 3:36 "He who believes in the Son (Jesus) has eternal life; but he who does not obey the Son shall not see life, but the wrath of God abides in him."*

TRADE YOUR SIN FOR HIS RIGHTEOUSNESS. - Say "Dear God I am a sinner. Forgive me. Thank you Jesus for dying on the cross; I receive what You did for me. I give you my sins and my life. I now receive You as my Savior and the Lord of my life. I receive eternal life and a home in Heaven. My trust for eternity is completely in You. I am now saved. God is now my Father; Heaven is now my home. In Jesus Name I pray. Amen. (Now get water baptized, read the Bible everyday, pray everyday, meet regularly with other believers, ask Jesus to baptize you in the Holy Spirit for power to live a life pleasing to Him and to tell others about Him. (Read Acts 2:38, Romans 3:10, 3:23, 5:8-9, 6:23, 10:9-10, 13, John 3:16, Luke 11:13, Mat. 10:32-33, Acts 1:8). Seek God for daily wisdom.

MAKE THE TRADE. - Trade your sorrows and shame for His joys. Trade your sickness and pain for His healing. Trade your worries for His peace. Trade your doubt for His faith. Trade your defeat for His victory. Trade your problems for His solutions. *And don't take them back - leave them with Him.*

chapter 18

Persistence

Luke 11:8 I tell you, even though he will not get up and give him anything because he is his friend, yet because of his persistence he will get up and give him as much as he needs.

The above verse is the end of a parable. It's a story about a man who wakes his friend up at night to get some food for another friend of his who has come on a journey to visit him. The story is from Luke 11:5-8 and the teaching on it continues in verses 9-13. The teaching is also in the book of Matthew. *Matthew 7:7 Ask and it shall be given to you; seek and you shall find; knock and it shall be opened to you. (8) For everyone who asks receives and he who seeks finds, and to him who knocks it shall be opened. (9) Or what man is there among you, when his son shall ask him for a loaf, will he give him a stone: (10) Or if he shall ask for a fish, he will not give him a snake, will he? (11) If you then, being evil, know how to give good gifts to your children, how much more shall your Father who is in heaven give what is good to those who ask Him!* (See also Luke 11:9-13) Luke 11:13 If you then, being evil, know how to give good gifts to your children, how much more shall your Heavenly Father give the Holy Spirit to those who ask Him?

You may say, "I've done that." Well, keep on asking, keep on seeking and keep on knocking.

In Mark 2:1-13, friends brought a paralytic to Jesus to be healed. They couldn't get in the door of the house so they let him down through a hole they made in the roof. They had **Persistence.** They were not giving up until they got what they came for. The result: *(verse 5) "And Jesus seeing their faith said to the paralytic,*

'My son, your sins are forgiven.'" Verse 11 "I say to you, rise and take up your pallet and go home. (12) And he rose and immediate- ly took up his pallet and went out in the sight of all;..." Thank God for friends that will help and persevere with you in prayer, who help you out, who won't give up, but will join their faith and **per- sistence** with yours.

And look at Bartimeus, a blind man, who received his sight when he came to Jesus. *Mark 10:46-52 (47) And when he heard that it was Jesus the Nazarene, he began to cry out and say, 'Jesus, Son of David, have mercy on me!' (48) And many were sternly telling him to be quiet, but he kept crying all the more, 'Son of David, have mercy on me!'"* Maybe you have been crying out to God for a long time. People around you have told you be quiet about it, stop asking God, quit all that believing, all of that confes- sion, all of that praising and praying. Well look at Bartimeus. He had <u>persistence</u>. He cried out all the more. The result - *(49) "Jesus stopped and said, 'Call him here.' (51) And answering him, Jesus said, 'What do you want me to do for you?' And the blind man said to Him, 'Rabboni, (my Master), I want to regain my sight!' (52) And Jesus said to him, 'Go your way; your faith has made you well.'* And immediately he regained his sight and began following him on the road." He got his healing quickly but it was his per- sistence that got Jesus' attention. So, He asked the man, "What do you want?" He wants for us to tell Him what we want, what we need, even though He already knows before we ask. The Holy Spirit will teach us how to pray about our situations, but we still need to ask, then believe and thank God for the supply or answer and receive it.

Many of you have trained barrel racing horses to become winners through sheer **persistence**; horses that could run but wouldn't turn. You went around those barrels enough times, over and over, until finally you had a winner on your hands. Your **per- sistence** paid off. It's the same with good calf roping horses. Many of the best ones were the hardest to train **but through persistence they became winners.** Some rodeo cowboys have less natural athletic ability than others **but because of persistence** to reach their goal, they are winning the money, buckles and saddles. They win with persistence.

Sometimes you may feel like quitting. Your biggest blessing may be right around the corner, coming soon. *Hebrews 10:35 "Therefore, do not throw away your confidence, which has a great reward. (36) For you have need of endurance (or patience) so that when you have done the will of God, you may receive what was promised. (39) But we are not of those who shrink back to destruction, but of those who have faith to preserving of the soul."* Also see James 1:2-4.

Hebrews 13:8 "Jesus Christ is the same yesterday, and today, yes and forever." He will do for you as He did for the paralytic and the blind man and the many, many that came to Him and **are still coming to Him. "Be persistent."** Get to Jesus. Cry out all the more. Keep asking, seeking and knocking. God will move on your behalf as He sees your faith.

And don't forget, Jesus is also knocking; He is knocking at your hearts door. Won't you let Him come in.

Persistence to Heaven: *Revelation 3:20 "Behold, I stand at the door and knock; if anyone hears My voice and opens the door, I will come in to him and will dine with him, and he with Me."* Be persistent enough to finish what you know God wants you to do. He wants you to have eternal life with Him in Heaven. Accept Jesus as Savior and Lord; open the door of your heart and life right now. Confess that you are a sinner and ask God to forgive you of all your sins and thank Him for doing it right now. Get Baptized, pray every day, read the Bible every day, fellowship (meet with) other believers regularly. (If you have any questions about this and your soul's destiny, read Romans 3:10, 3:23, 5:8-9, 6:23; 10:9-10 and John 3:3-8, John 3:16 and Mark 16:15-16 and I John

5:11-13. If you are Christian already but have not turned everything over to the Lord, open all the doors to your heart and life and let Jesus take charge and be Lord of all. Pray and do it right now. **Be Persistent!**

chapter
19

Restoring Broken Dreams And Visions

Acts 2:17-18 "And it shall be in the last days, God says, 'that I will pour forth of My Spirit upon all mankind; and your sons and daughters shall prophecy and your young men shall see visions, and your old men shall dream dreams; Even on my bondslaves, both men and women, I will in those days pour forth of My spirit and they shall prophesy."

Note, for the older ones: It says, old men dream dreams. God would not give you a dream if He did not want you to complete it. Don't give up because of your age. *Psalm 92:14 "They shall still bear fruit in old age; they shall be fresh (full of sap or oil which represents the anointing and power of the Holy Spirit) and flourishing (green, full of life and producing)." See Joel 2:33 "So I will restore to you the years that the swarming locust has eaten..."*

Many of you have had dreams and visions placed in your spirit by the Spirit of God and (1) never have taken any steps to complete them (2) some of you have started to complete them, but discouragement set in because of lack of help, lack of money and/or lack of success in the early going, (3) a set back has caused you to give up on your God given dreams and destiny (4) Some have given up on your dreams, because you let "the desire for other things enter in and choke the word." Like the seed sown among thorns in Mark 4:18-19 (5) some have started to fulfill their dreams and visions. Things were going good and in the right direction. Then a dream stealer of some kind caused it to crumble. All of these reasons and more have caused you to have <u>broken dreams.</u>

Hebrews 13:8 "Jesus Christ is the same yesterday and today, yes and forever." He is still the healer of broken hearts, broken bodies and broken dreams. At the cross he took care of every need we ever needed.

Phil. 1:6 "For I am confident of this very thing that He (God) who began a good work in you will perfect it until the day of Christ Jesus."

In the Old Testament in Genesis 37 God began a good work in Joseph. He began it in dreams. In verse 7 the dream showed his brothers sheaves (bundles of wheat) stood around and bowed down to his sheaf in the field. (8) His brothers hated him for his dreams and his words - they said "shall you indeed reign over us." In verse 28 we see that his brothers sold him into slavery. End of dream so it seemed.

But God is the One who had given Joseph that dream. God is in control in this earth. But it got worse and Joseph ended up in prison. One thing Joseph did though - He kept his heart and actions right with God. Refusing to have sex with his Master's (Potiphar's) wife landed him in prison by false accusation. It seemed the dream was even further away from completion now. However, God caused Joseph to fulfill his dream. He came out of prison to become the second highest ranking ruler in the nation. His brothers did bow to him. He was able to keep his father, brothers and their families from starvation. By doing this he preserved all Israel.

Read Ps. 106:16-22 for a summary. *Verse 19 says "Until*

the time that his word came to pass, the word of the Lord tested him (Joseph) (20) The king sent and released him, the ruler of the people let him go free (21) He made him lord of his house, and ruler of his possessions..."

Job 33:15-18 In a dream, in a vision of the night, when deep sleep falls upon men, while slumbering on their beds, (16) Then He (God) opens the ears of men, and seals their instruction. (17) In order to turn man from his deed, and conceal pride from man, (18) He keeps back his soul from the pit, and his life from perishing by the sword.

What dream - what vision has God placed in your spirit, in your mind, in you heart? Write it down and press on to fulfill it!

Habakkuk 2:2-3 "Then the LORD answered me and said: "Write the vision and make it plain on tablets, that he may run who reads it. (3) For the vision is yet for an appointed time; But at the end it will speak, and it will not lie. Though it tarries, wait for it; because it will surely come, it will not tarry."

Guard your mind. Cast down imaginations that don't line up with your God given destiny. *"Take every thought captive to the obedience of Christ. "* II Cor. 10:3-5.

God told Paul to go preach the gospel in Rome. Paul had a shipwreck on the way but he did go to Rome. He fulfilled his purpose.

Jesus had a vision to see us in heaven so he went to the cross and died, then rose again, so we can go be with Him in heaven and have eternal life.

Guard, and fulfill your dreams by doing what God says to do completely, when He says to do it and how He says to do it.

Fulfill Jesus dreams. For the joy set before Jesus, He went to the cross to reconcile us to the Father. We are His joy. Fulfill His and your joy by receiving eternal life through Christ Jesus. Pray - I am a sinner who needs a Savior. Thank you Jesus for dying for me on the cross and shedding your blood to wash my sins away. I receive You, Jesus, right now into my life to be my Savior and Lord of my life. My new vision in life is now to serve you and one day be united with You in heaven for all eternity. I now call God my Father. Holy Spirit help me to complete the destiny God has for me in the earth until I see You face to face. In Jesus Name. Amen.

Now read Romans 3:10, 3:23, 5:8-9, 6:23, 10:9-10, 13, Acts 1:8, Acts 2:38, John 3:16, Luke 11:13. Get water baptized, ask Jesus to baptize you in the Holy Spirit, read the Bible daily, pray daily, meet with other believers often.

chapter

20

Sanctify And Consecrate

Hebrews 10:10 "By this will (the will of God to establish the New Covenant) we have been sanctified through the offering of the body of Jesus Christ once for all."

The word sanctify means - "set apart." When we receive Jesus as Savior and Lord, He sets us apart from sin, from the world's way of doing things and from our old lifestyle. He sets us apart to go to heaven instead of hell. He sets us apart to be a light in a dark world. He sets us apart to do good works and glorify the Father.

Isaiah 61 says, we are anointed by the Holy Ghost to preach the good news, to set people free, to proclaim the second coming of Jesus Christ, to give people beauty for ashes, the oil of joy for mourning and to give a garment of praise to remove the spirit of heaviness that they might be called "trees of righteousness." Jesus died and washed our sins away so we can be righteous (in right standing) before God, the Father. *II Cor. 5:21 "He made Him who knew no sin to be sin on our behalf, that we might become the righteousness of God in Christ."*

Jesus did not save us so we could go on living in sin - in a sinful lifestyle. Being a Christian is not just to pray for forgiveness, confess Jesus as Lord to others and then go out and party with the world for the next twenty years. *James 4:4 "...whoever wishes to be a friend of the world makes himself an enemy of God."* (This means the way or system of the world - man's sinful way over God's way).

Those who came to Jesus, came one way and left another. They repented (changed directions). They went from hate to love, greed to generosity, meanness to kindness, sickness to good health, gloom to joy, ungodly living to holiness.

I Cor. 6:9-11 "Or do you not know that the unrighteous will not inherit the kingdom of God? Do not be deceived; neither fornicators, nor idolaters, nor adulterers, nor effeminate, nor homosexuals, (10) nor thieves, nor the covetous, nor drunkards, nor revilers, nor swindlers, will inherit the kingdom of God. (11) Such were some of you; but you were washed, but you were sanctified, but you were justified in the name of the Lord Jesus Christ and in the Spirit of our God."

The Bible uses words like justified, sanctified, glorified and also there is the word consecrated.

Justified - God sees us just as if we never sinned. (Romans 5:5)

Sanctified - set apart by God to live a life for God. (I Cor. 6:11)

Glorified - to become like Jesus. One day we will have glorified bodies and live forever.

Now I would like to present another word we don't hear very often.

Consecrated - this also means set apart, but we are the ones who do it. People who set themselves apart from ungodly lifestyles are living a consecrated life. In Exodus 13:1-2 God told Moses to "Consecrate to Me all the first born...it is Mine." They set aside the firstborn animal and the firstfruits of their crops and offered it to God. This signifies that God has first place in our lives and in everything.

God sets us apart to bless us. Some people seem to be able

to walk in the blessings more than others. They keep their peace and joy; they love people and are loved; their lives prosper, they have battles but they come through in victory. They don't sin and fall for temptation as easily as others. <u>The reason</u> - they have chosen to live a consecrated lifestyle before God and man. They still love their old friends - they just can't run with them.

So here it is. God sets you apart for blessing when you receive Jesus as Savior - <u>but the blessing comes when you consecrate or set yourself apart to live for God.</u> Everyone wants a Savior so they can go to heaven and not hell - but everyone does not want a Lord. Lord means Adonai, Master, Boss. It means "I am going to do it Jesus' way and not mine."

Receiving Jesus makes you a child of God. When you consecrate yourself to God you become "<u>sons and daughters.</u>" You grow up. You become mature. *II Cor. 6:17 says, "Therefore come out from their midst and be separate" says the Lord. And do not touch what is unclean; and I will welcome you, (18) "And I will be a Father to you and you shall be sons and daughters to me" says the Lord Almighty.*

Matthew 25 says that one day God will put the sheep (His people) on the right; He will put the goats (those who do not receive Him) on the left. Those on the right receive eternal rewards; those on the left receive eternal punishments.

To enjoy the abundant life Jesus provides here and the eternal life He gives, make the decision to consecrate your life for God.

Be Set Apart For Eternity - Pray: Dear God I am a sinner I ask you to forgive me. I am ready to set myself apart to live for you and do your will. I believe Jesus died on the cross and rose on the third day to set me apart for heaven and for godly living now. I receive Jesus as my Lord and Savior at this moment. I receive eternal life. I make a commitment to serve you, to consecrate my life to live for you. Thank you that heaven is now my home. I can call God my Father. Holy Spirit help me live a life pleasing to my Father in heaven. In Jesus Name I pray. *Romans 10:13 "Whoever calls on the name of the Lord shall be saved."* (Now read Romans 3:10, 3:23, 5:8-9, 10:9-10, 13, John 3:16, Acts 1:8, Acts 2:38)

chapter

21

Stay Focused

Hebrews 12:2 *"Fixing our eyes on Jesus, the author and per-fector of faith, who for the joy set before Him endured the cross, despising the shame, and has sat down at the right hand of the throne of God."*

Our Focus is to be on Jesus. He is the Savior and Lord of all. He is our greatest example of how to live in this world. He "always" shunned evil and lived righteously. He was not concerned about "doing his own thing," or about flirting with any sin, but He was always concerned about doing the Father's will. He not only came to die for us but came to live for us to show us how to live by faith in God and His word. When we do it Jesus way, we will not fail. Looking to, and <u>staying focused</u> on Jesus will give us faith and cause us to grow in faith as we proceed from battle to battle and victory to victory.

In the Book of Deuteronomy, Chapter 28, there is a list of blessings that are ours, including our cattle, our work, our supplies, our children if we "diligently obey God and keep His commandments." *Deut. 28:14 says, "So you shall not turn aside from any of the words which I command you this day, to the right or to the left, to go after other gods to serve them."*

Anything or anyone you trust more than God becomes your god. - When we do things God's way it opens us up for blessings, but it takes effort to stay focused. It requires dedication, perseverance and it involves making a decision. And making it over and over again so you will not be swayed, distracted or be deterred. It's being the best we can be for God.

We must stay focused on Jesus, and on the Word of God, because there are so many temptations, so many distractions, so many tests and trials. If we do not stay focused on doing what is right, good and true, we will fail.

Watch the successful World Champions and perennial contestants at the National Finals Rodeo. Watch what they do, what they talk about, watch their faces, watch their eyes. They are so determined to win - so focused - they continue to win. They are not distracted. Their attitude - "I'm here to win - nothing will deter me."

Remember the lady (in Matthew 9:20-22) with the hemorrhage for 12 years. She was determined to get to Jesus. She was focused on the hem of His garment for she was saying to herself, "If I only touch His garment (His cloak) I shall get well." She touched it, and Jesus said in vs 22, "...your faith has made you well." At once the woman was made well!

Remember Jesus, who is our best example to follow. Already at 12 years of age He was focused. He said, "I must be about My Father's business." He was determined to die for us and take our sins on Himself so we do not have to carry them. He would not let people or the pain that He endured distract Him. Isaiah 50:7 says "He set His face like a flint." - knowing God would help Him."

The Bible says that Jesus, "resolutely set His face to go to Jerusalem ". He was determined to get you and me to Heaven. He had to die to do it - nothing would deter Him.

Hebrews 12:2 above says "who for the joy set before Him endured the cross." We, me and you, are that joy. He would rather die than live without us. So He focused on the only thing

He could do to get us to Heaven - death on a cross to provide forgiveness for us and eternal life in Heaven. So now it's up to us to focus on Him.

How do we stay focused on the things of God? We read His Word, the Bible, and we pray daily. We meet with other believers often. We shun sin. We stay away from people and things and activities that distract us from being what God wants us to be. We get serious about God. We chose God's way always. We are led by the Holy Spirit in everything we do.

Jesus was focused on us to get us to Heaven - now it's up to us to receive Him. John 1:12 "But as many as received Him, to them He gave the right to become the children of God, even to those who believe in His name." If you want to receive Jesus, pray this, "Dear God, I am a sinner, I need a Savior. Forgive my sins, come into my heart, come into my life. I receive Jesus now as my Savior and Lord. I receive eternal life; I receive Heaven as my home. Thank you Jesus for staying focused on the cross; I will now stay focused on You forever. Holy Spirit, help me stay focused on pleasing my Father God in heaven. In Jesus name, Amen. Read John 3:16, Luke 3:16, Luke 11:13, Romans 8:14, Romans 10:9 & 10, Acts 2:38, II Peter 3:18.

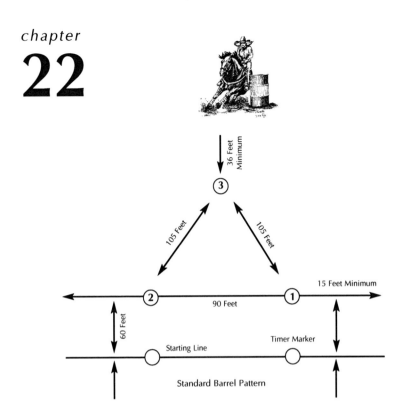

36 Feet Minimum

③

105 Feet   105 Feet

② — 90 Feet — ①   15 Feet Minimum

60 Feet

Starting Line   Timer Marker

Standard Barrel Pattern

The Correct Pattern And The Proper Order

There is a correct pattern and a proper order for us to live by.

Exodus 25.9 (God told Moses) "According to all that I show you, that is, the pattern of the tabernacle and the pattern of all its furnishings, just so shall you make it."

God told them exactly how the tabernacle would be made and how it would look. He gave them the correct pattern and He gives us the correct pattern for our lives.

The tabernacle was a tent dedicated to God for His presence and glory. Later, King Solomon built a permanent temple dedicated to God for His presence and glory. Today, when you receive Jesus, your body becomes a temple of the Holy Spirit. *I Corinthians 3:16-17 "Do you not know that you are temple of God, and that the Spirit of God dwells in you? (17) If any man destroys the temple of God, God will destroy him, for the temple of God is holy, and that is what you are."*

We also need to dedicate our temple, our body, to God for His presence and glory to shine through. We are to be light in a dark world. The presence of God brings forth light. Darkness represents sin and evil; light represents clean thoughts, actions and righteousness (right standing with God). When others are in our presence, they should sense or know or feel the presence of God in us. There is a joy in God's presence. *Psalm 16:11 "In Your presence is fullness of joy..."* Also in His presence is victory, strength, wisdom, deliverance, power and rest.

Moses understood the importance of God's presence. God told Moses, "My Presence will go with you and I will give you rest." (Exodus 33:14) and Moses responded (verse 15) "...If Your Presence does not go with us, do not bring us up from here." In other words - "If You are not going, I am not going!"

For our life now - Jesus is our pattern. *Hebrews 12:2 "fixing our eyes on Jesus, the author and perfector of our faith..."*

Jesus was always concerned about doing the Father's will. Jesus always walked in love. Jesus never sinned. Jesus always lived in victory. We are to be like Him. Romans 8:29 says we are to be conformed to His image.

One example of running the correct pattern is the Barrel Racing event. It is a cloverleaf pattern, one right and two lefts or one left and two rights. You must run the correct pattern to win. In life, we must run the correct pattern to receive blessings. Run in such a way that you may win. (I Corinthians 9:24). Run for the eternal life which is found in knowing Jesus as your Savior and

Lord. He is our imperishable prize.

When we don't run the correct pattern we get penalized and when we do, we get rewarded. Romans 6:23 "For the wages of sin is death, but the free gift of God is eternal life in Christ Jesus our Lord."

God does not want to penalize you - He wants to reward you. The choice is yours. Choose Jesus, choose blessings, choose life!

Also, there is a proper order. The Levites were the only tribe God allowed to touch the tabernacle and the ark of the covenant. There was a proper order of how to transport and take care of the ark. Because of Israel's disobedience, and lack of honor for God, He allowed the enemy to steal the ark. They knew the power of God was in it for the Israelites. Later, King David brought the ark of God back. The first time he tried, they did not handle the ark the way God instructed them to. I Chronicles 13:8-10. It was supposed to be carried by the Levites with poles on their shoulders. Instead, they were trying to return it on a cart pulled by oxen. The oxen stumbled, and a man named Uzza, reached out his hand to steady the ark. "God struck him because he put his hand to the ark; and he died there before God" You may say that sounds too drastic, but God is serious about His orders to us. A few months later David sent for the ark again. The Priests told him, in I Chronicles 15:13, "For because you did not do it the first time, the Lord our God broke out against us, because we did not consult Him about the proper order." (regarding the ordinance): This time the priests and the Levites bore the ark of God on their shoulders, by poles, as Moses commanded, and the ark was returned and there was great rejoicing. Remember, when the ark was carried into battle the Israelites won major victories because of God's Presence among them.

One more story about order. II Kings 20:1, (Isaiah, the

prophet, said to King Hezekiah), "Thus says the Lord, 'Set your house in order, for you shall die, and not live.'" Hezekiah prayed and God added 15 years to his life. The Bible records that Hezekiah did that which was good, right and true and he sought God with all his heart and so he prospered. His relationship with God was in order and his prayer for his life was answered.

You cannot clean up your own act. You cannot put yourself in order permanently. God created you. Get Him involved in your life. The blood of Jesus will wash you clean and set you in proper relationship with God.

How do you set your House (Your life) in order?

(#1) Confess your sin (I John 1:9) (#2) Ask forgiveness (#3) Repent - turn away from sin and turn to God (#4) Receive Jesus as Savior and the Lord (the Master, the Boss) of your life. (#5) You will run the correct pattern by following the Holy Ghost. (Romans 8:14) If this is your desire pray this prayer. "I'm a sinner, I need a Savior. Forgive me Lord of all my sins. I turn away from them, I repent, and I turn to You God. I receive Jesus right now as my Savior and Lord. Thank you for dying for me and washing my sin away with Your shed blood. Thank you for making a way for me to go to Heaven and have life eternally. Holy Spirit help me to live a life pleasing to my Father in Heaven. I am now saved. I love you Lord. In Jesus name. Now get baptized, read your Bible everyday, pray everyday. Meet often with other believers and grow in Christ.

The Fire

And The Power
(Baptism in the Holy Spirit And Fire)

Luke 3:16 John the Baptist said, "As for me, I baptize you with water; but One is coming who is mightier than I, and I am not fit to untie the thong of His sandals; He will baptize you with the Holy Spirit and fire."

We need the fire of God in our lives. The Holy Spirit and fire of God will give you power to be an overcomer, to live a godly life, to defeat the devil. You will be a bold witness. You will see signs, wonders, miracles, the gifts of the Holy Spirit. You will have bigger battles, but you will have more power to be victorious.

It is one thing to have a measure of the Holy Spirit in you. It is another to have "the Spirit without measure", that Jesus gives. See John 3:34. When Jesus baptizes you in the Holy Spirit to over-filling, you will be a changed person - more bold for the gospel. You will see more healings, more miracles, you will speak with authority over evil spirits, and they will go. You will speak to pain in bodies - it will go. You will speak to situations - they will change. You will speak life wherever you go.

Have you ever noticed that some people seem to be stronger in God, in their walk and talk? They <u>speak with authori-</u>

ty. They don't fall for temptation as easy. They resist the devil - he flees (James 4:7) They use the name of Jesus with authority.

Do you want this? You need to ask Jesus to baptize you in the Holy Spirit and fire. The Holy spirit convicts you of sin, so you will confess it and be forgiven. The Holy Spirit points you to Jesus. The Holy Spirit will lead, guide and protect you. The Holy Spirit will pray with you. The Holy Spirit will give you the boldness you need to win in life and serve God to the fullest.

And you need the fire. The fire of God will burn out the junk and sin in your life. The fire of God will fire you up to serve Jesus. He will give you a tongue of fire.

An Old Testament example of this is Isaiah. In *Is. 6:5-8, Isaiah went from "Woe is me, for I am undone! Because I am a man of unclean lips..." to "Here I am! Send me."* This was after the angel touched his lips with a live coal from the altar in heaven.

The same thing happened to the disciples and the rest of the 120, including Mary, the mother of Jesus, on the day of Pentecost, fifty days after the crucifixion of Jesus.

Acts 2:1-4 "When the day of Pentecost had come, they were all together in one place. (2) And suddenly there came from heaven a noise like a violent rushing wind, and it filled the whole house where they were sitting. (3) And there appeared to them tongues as of fire distributing themselves, and they rested on each one of them. (4) And they were all filled with the Holy Spirit and began to speak with other tongues, as the Spirit was giving them utterance."

They went from hiding in fear, to preaching in the streets with boldness. Three thousand were saved the first sermon. Another five thousand received Jesus the second sermon and the church grew in numbers day by day.

Acts 2 says they spoke in tongues as the Spirit was giving

them utterance. Acts 2:39 says, "the promise is for you and your children, and for all who are far off, as many as the Lord God shall call to Himself." We are afar off. And we can receive the outpouring and baptism in the Holy Spirit just as they did 2,000 years ago. <u>Jesus Christ is still baptizer in the Holy Ghost.</u>

You may not understand the gifts of the Holy Spirit such as speaking or praying in tongues, the interpretation of tongues, prophesying, healing, miracles and more. **<u>But you know one thing - you need more of God in your life.</u>** If that is you, ask Jesus to baptize you in the Holy Spirit and fire.

The Holy Spirit will come upon you and give you greater power to serve God. The fire will burn up all that is not pleasing to God. The fire will fire you up to serve God in a more powerful way. Also, the fire of God will burn those up for eternity, who do not receive His Son, Jesus Christ. Our God is a consuming fire. See Mat. 3:12, Heb. 10:26-31, Heb. 12:29

In Acts 2, Acts 8, Acts 10 and Acts 19 they all spoke in tongues when the Holy Spirit came upon them. You will too.

It may seem strange. This is because the Bible says, in 1 Cor. 14, it is a "mystery". It also says you are speaking to God, not to men. It always edifies, (builds you up) so you can build others up. Jude 20 says that when you pray in the Spirit you build yourselves up on your most holy faith. *Romans 8:26 says "we do not know how to pray as we should but the Spirit Himself prays for us (in us) with groanings to deep for words."*

Sometimes, our spirit is trying to call out to God and we do not even know how to express ourselves, so we pray in tongues for the breakthrough we need. Our spirit talks to the Holy Spirit. We bypass our brains and speak directly to God in tongues.

You will be more confident and bold when you are baptized in the Holy Spirit.

When Jesus was baptized in the Holy Spirit, in Mat. 3:16,

He began His public ministry of signs, wonders, miracles, casting out demons and speaking with authority.

Peter denied knowing Jesus at His trial, the night before they crucified Him. But, at Pentecost, when the Holy Spirit fell upon Peter, he was a changed man. Threats, beatings and imprisonment could not stop him from preaching about Jesus. (See Acts 4:18-20).

There are nine gifts of the Holy Spirit. You will experience all, or some of them. See 1 Cor. 12:8-10. They are word of wisdom, word of knowledge, faith, gifts of healing, effecting of miracles, prophecy, discerning of spirits, various kinds of tongues and the interpretation of tongues.

<u>Settle your eternity plus receive the Power of the Holy Spirit.</u> Pray. Dear God, I am a sinner, forgive me. I accept Jesus now as my Savior and Lord of my life. Thank You for washing my sins away with Your blood on the cross. Thank You for eternal life. Jesus, baptize me in the Holy Spirit and fire. Burn out the junk and sinful lifestyle. Fire me up to serve you and bring others to know you. In Jesus Name I pray. Amen.

The Right Path

Psalm 107:7 "And He (God) led them forth by the right way, that they might go to a city for a dwelling place."

God will lead you in "the right way." When you are in the right way battles and troubles still come but, it does not discourage you, because you know you are in God's will; and you know you are in the right way, so you continue through each battle to victory. If we are not in the right way, then we give ground or access for the devil to attack, and cause havoc and defeat in our lives. We need to get in prayer and the reading of God's Word. Get honest with self and God. If your troubles are because you are on the wrong path for this particular season of your life - then seek God for the right path. He will be glad once He knows you are willing to change and He will put you on the right path. Remember, you can do a good thing, and you will see some fruit from your efforts, but is it the best thing? What you have done before may have been right for a particular season of your life, but is it the best for this season.

Remember, Paul was told by God to go to Rome. He had a shipwreck on the way, but he did make it to Rome and accomplished God's purpose in his life there. However, many of the shipwrecks of life we encounter are because we are not going where God says, or we are unwilling to go and to do what God is saying to us in this season.

Good news - God will lead us in the right path. Get this down. God will lead us in the right path. He always has our best interest at heart. Be confident in that. One thing we can do in this earth, is trust God. Trust Him and rest in peace as you seek Him - He will lead you in the right path, just for you, and there will be peace and blessings in the right path. Battles - yes; defeat - no.

Romans 8:14 "For all who are being led by the Spirit of God, these are sons of God."

Isaiah 55:6 "Seek the Lord while He may be found, call upon Him while He is near."

Saul of Tarsus, who became Paul the apostle, was going on the wrong road to Damascus to persecute, kill and jail people for being Christians. Jesus appeared to Him and changed his direction in life. He became one of the most outspoken believers for Jesus, in his day, and wrote many of the books in the New Testament. When God put him on the right path, he was able to fulfill his purpose in life, and show many how to receive eternal life in Jesus Christ.

The Bible says in *Romans 10:14 "How shall they call upon Him in whom they have not believed?..." You need to know God personally to call upon Him for "the right path for your life."*

The Right Path For Believers.

If you already know Jesus as Savior and Lord keep seeking Him. You will get the answer for the right path to be on if you are willing to go on any path He takes you. You may not understand the path, you may resist the path at first, you may want to go on anoth-

83

er path, but go on the right path - the Holy Spirit leads you on - <u>it is the path of blessings</u>.

The Right Path to Heaven

Some say pray to the God of your choice and we will pray to the God of our choice. The Bible declares very clearly as noted in the Number One Commandment in Deut. 6:4 and Mark 11:29 that there in only one Lord and also that there is only one way, one right path to the Father in Heaven. *John 14:6 "Jesus said to him 'I am the way, and the truth, and the life; no one comes to the Father, but through Me.'"* Are you on the right path to eternal life in Heaven. You can be. If you are willing and it is your desire, pray this. "Dear God, I am a sinner, I need a Savior, forgive me of all my sins, put me on the right path to heaven; I ask Jesus who is the only way to You to come into my heart and life and be my Savior and the Lord of my life. I turn away from the path of sin and I turn to You. Thank You Jesus for making a way for me to have eternal life. God is now my Father. Holy Spirit help me to lead a life pleasing to my Father in Heaven. In Jesus name I pray." Read John 3:3; 3:6, 3:16, Luke 3:16; Luke 11:13, Romans 8:14, Romans 10:9 & 10, Acts 1:8. Get baptized. Read the Bible and pray daily to stay on a right path. Get involved in church. Meet regularly with other believers.

chapter

25

The

Tree Of Life

Genesis 2:9 "And out of the ground the Lord God made every tree grow that is pleasant to the sight and good for food. The tree of life was also in the midst of the garden, and the tree of knowledge of good and evil."

The tree of life is mentioned in the first book of the Bible, Genesis, and toward the middle, in Proverbs, and again in the last book of Revelation.

There were two trees in the middle of the Garden of Eden. God always gives us a choice. We have a free will; Choose God, receive His Son Jesus Christ as our Savior and have eternal life or reject Him and go off to torment in hell forever. We can speak life/choose life or we can speak death/choose death. *Proverbs 18:21 "Death and life are in the power of the tongue, and those who love it will eat its fruit."*

Deut. 30:15 See I have set before you today life and good, death and evil; (16) In that I command you today to love the Lord your God, to walk in His ways, and to keep His commandments,

His statutes, His judgments, that you may live and multiply; and the Lord your God will bless you in the land which you go to possess." Verse 19 says "...therefore choose life, that both you and your descendants may live."

You will go toward your dominant thought. You will move toward sin and away from God - or - you will move toward God and righteousness.

James 4:7 "Submit to God. Resist the devil and he will flee from you (8) Draw near to God and He will draw near to you..."

As mentioned earlier - God always gives us choice.

Genesis 2:8 "The Lord planted a garden eastward in Eden and there He put the man whom He had formed. (9) And out of the ground the Lord God made every tree grow that is pleasant to the sight and good for food. The tree of life was also in the midst of the garden, and the tree of the knowledge of good and evil." (16) "And the Lord God commanded the man, saying, "Of every tree of the garden you may freely eat; (17) but of the tree of the knowledge of good and evil you shall not eat, for in the day that you eat of it you shall surely die."

Then, we see how sin entered the world, by Eve and through Adam.

In Genesis 3:1-13, we see that the serpent (the devil, Satan) deceived Eve by telling her that if she ate of the tree of knowledge of good and evil she would be like God, and she would not die.

Eve saw it, she desired/lusted for it, then she took it. That is what gets us into trouble and sin. We see, we lust, we take or partake - sin enters.

Then, only the blood of Jesus, with His gift of grace, washes our sin away, when we confess our sin. (See I John 1:7-9)

Immediately, in Genesis 3:15, God had a plan to send Jesus, the seed of the woman; a virgin birth would produce the Savior of the world. (Women do not have seed.) This Savior is

Jesus; He would defeat the devil and bring us back in good standing with God. This is for <u>all who receive</u> the Savior, Jesus Christ as Lord.

John 3:36 "He who believes in the Son (Jesus) has eternal life; but he who does not obey the Son shall not see life but the wrath of God abides on him."

Next we see the tree of life mentioned in *Proverbs 11:30 "The fruit of the righteous is a tree of life, and he who wins souls is wise."*

The next book we see the tree of life mentioned, is in the book of Revelation, at the end of the Bible. Read Revelation 2:1-7. *Rev. 2:3, "and you have perseverance and have endured for My name's sake and have not grown weary. (4) But, I have this against you, that you have left your first love (5) Remember therefore from where you have fallen, and repent and do the deeds you did at first; or else I am coming to you, and will remove your lampstand out of its place - unless you repent. (7) He who has an ear, let him hear what the Spirit says to the churches. To him who overcomes, I will grant to eat of the tree of life, which is in the garden of God."*

Then, in the last book and chapter in the Bible, Revelation 22, we see the tree of life again.

Rev. 22:1-2 & 14 (1) "Then he showed me a river of the water of life, clear as crystal, coming from the throne of God and of the Lamb, (2) in the middle of its street. On either side of the river was the tree of life, bearing twelve kinds of fruit, yielding its fruit every month; and the leaves of the tree were for the healing of the nations. (14) Blessed are those who wash their robes, so that they may have the right to the tree of life, and may enter by the gates into the city."

Good news!!! We will eat of the tree of life that Adam and Eve could have eaten of and had life. If they had chosen God's way, and had eaten of the tree of life, they would have never died and sin would not have entered into all of us. The devil could have been kicked out of the Garden of Eden, instead of Adam and Eve.

By faith in God, let's choose His ways. Choose life and expect and receive blessings in this life.

So now it is up to us to choose life and not death. Choose Jesus - He is the way of life eternal, the way to the Father in Heaven, the way to Heaven.

John 14:6 "Jesus said to him, 'I am the way, and the truth, and the life; no one comes to the Father but through Me.'"

Pray: God, forgive me of my sins; I choose to turn away from sinful living to You. I choose to receive Jesus as my Savior and Lord. Thank you Jesus for dying for me and taking my sin away. Wash me clean by the blood You shed for me. I choose to live as You desire me to live - I choose life - I choose Jesus. I choose to listen to and obey the Holy Spirit who now lives in me. God - you are now my Father, Jesus is my Lord; Heaven is my home. In Jesus Name. I pray, Amen.

Now get water baptized, ask Jesus to baptize you in the Holy Spirit, read your Bible daily, pray daily, meet with other believers often, confess Jesus before others, and serve God. Read Romans 3:10; 3:23; 5:8-9; 6:23, 10:9-10, 13; John 3:16; Acts 1:8; Acts 2:38.

chapter 26
The Way Of Escape

I Cor. 10:13 "No temptation has overtaken you, but such as is common to man; and God is faithful, who will not allow you to be tempted beyond what you are able, but with the temptation will provide the way of escape also, that you may be able to endure it."

For any situation, sin, trap, temptation, problem, bondage, addiction, or anything else you feel captured by, God has provided for you and me, "the way of escape."

We all have our strengths and weaknesses. "...the devil prowls like a roaring lion, seeking someone to devour." (See I Peter 5:2) He is prowling, looking for your weak spot, any door he can get an entrance into your thinking and your life. The devil has a lot of schemes. We must not fear him, but we should be aware of him and his schemes to steal, kill and destroy our lives.

For some, the devil tempts with partying and sex; for others it is drugs, still others alcohol. Also, there is unforgiveness, bitterness, not putting God first in your life, rebellion, jealousy, pride, eating disorders, depression, the cares of this world, homosexuality, fear, wasting time and other schemes. Remember the devil is a liar. When we abide in God's Word, it brings forth truth and it will set you free and keep you free. The more truth you have in you the quicker you will recognize a lie. So, read the Word often, listen to anointed men of God preach and teach. Live the Word and Jesus will set you free indeed. (See John 8:31-32, 36).

First off, when you know your weakness or sin, ask God to help you by giving you understanding and strengthening you in that area. Ask Him to help you with any temptation. Find promises and Scriptures pertaining to it. If you have unforgiveness in your heart, then eat forgiveness Scriptures and study the bad result and consequence of unforgiveness. If you don't forgive others, God won't forgive you. (Mat. 6:14-15, Mark 11:25-26) Choose to forgive - your feelings will catch up later. In II Cor. 2:10-11, Paul knew unforgiveness would separate him from God's forgiveness. So, he chose to forgive and, verse 11 says, "in order that no advantage be taken of us by Satan; for we are not ignorant of his schemes."

If you are constantly under bodily attack with sickness - eat healing Scriptures until you see the hand of God restore you to health. If you have lustful thoughts and actions, eat Scriptures concerning the consequences and also the blessings for staying pure and holy before God. If you have pride, eat Scriptures on being humble, then God will exalt you. Whatever your problem there is an answer for it in God's word and God who is faithful will provide the way of escape.

Sometimes, you may have to get help from good books, counselors, friends or others you meet to get some practical help and understanding. Listen carefully and be teachable. Remember, never do anything contradictory to the Word of God; with any teaching or counsel you receive make sure it lines up with the Word. Then you apply wisdom to your understanding and get victory and be set free to walk in God's blessings.

When Jesus was tempted in the desert by Satan, Jesus spoke the Scriptures for every temptation. He submitted Himself to God. He resisted the devil and the devil did flee. (See Mat. 4:1-11 and James 4:7).

The Bible says, that we are to give no place to the devil. Ask the Holy Spirit to show you any entrance or doors you have opened or failed to shut that would give the evil one an entrance to your spirit, soul or body. Get wisdom! Get understanding! Get instruction! Repent! Then shut the door forever.

Also there are times you may be under attack for doing what is right - even for preaching the gospel. Paul and Silas were. They were put in jail. Their way of escape was praying and singing praises to God. They not only were delivered from jail, but were able to lead the jailer and his whole household to receive Jesus as Savior, thereby giving their family the way of escape from an eternity in hell.

Everyday people die. Some go to heaven. Some go to hell. Jesus is the way of escape from hell. His shedding of blood on the cross for our forgiveness, His death and resurrection provided all of us a way of escape from hell. *John 3:36 "He who believes in the Son (Jesus) has eternal life; but he who does not obey the Son shall not see life, but the wrath of God abides in him."* Hell was not designed for men, but for the devil and his fallen angels, so don't go there. All have sinned. Sin separates people from God. While we were still sinners, Christ died for us. The Bible says, *"the wages of sin is death but the free gift of God is eternal life through Jesus Christ our Lord." (Romans 6:23)* Jesus is the way of escape from hell and is the way to eternal life in Heaven. *John 14:6 "I am the way, the truth and the life; no one comes to the Father, but through Me."*

The Way Of Escape: Settle your eternal destiny now with a prayer like this. "God in Heaven, I am a sinner and I need a Savior. Thank you for providing a way of escape for me out of hell. Forgive my sins. I receive Jesus as my Savior and Lord of my life right now. Come into my heart Lord Jesus. Thank you for making a way for me to have eternal life with you and walk free from my sins, free from my past. Deliver me from every temptation. Holy Spirit show me how to live a life pleasing to my Father in Heaven. I am set free, I am saved! Thank You Jesus, I love You. In Jesus Name." *Romans 10:13 "Whoever shall call on the name of the Lord shall be saved."* Now get baptized, read the Bible everyday, pray everyday, meet regularly with other Christians. STAY FREE!

There Is A Blessing In Your Hands! - Use Them!

Mark 16_17-18 "And these signs will accompany those who have believed: in My name they will cast out demons, they will speak with new tongues; ((18) they will pick up serpents, and if they drink any deadly poison, it will not hurt them; they will lay hands on the sick, and they will recover."

Jesus often touched people to bless them and to heal them. We are to do the same. *In John 14:12 Jesus says, "Truly, truly, I say to you, he who believes in Me, the works that I do shall he do also; and greater works than these shall he do; because I go to the Father."* We are to do what He did.

He touched the unclean, the lepers, the sick, the brokenhearted, the children and the people who followed HIm. He watched them recover in every area of their lives.

Your hands were made to be a blessing. They are not there just to put food in your mouth and take care of your own needs. There is the anointing of God in your hands.

A few ways to use your hands are:

1) Hands are made to do work. *Deut. 28:8 and 12 says God will bless the work of your hands. And Eccles 9:10 "Whatever your*

hand find to do, do it with your might;..."

2) Clap for God - *Ps. 47:1 "O clap your hands, all you people! Shout to God with the voice of triumph!"* Applaud God!

3) Praise and Worship - *I Timothy 2:8 I want men in every place to pray, lifting up holy hands, without wrath and dissension."*

4) Help others - Look out for the interest of others. Phil 2:4, Gal. 6:2

5) For blessings to flow through, Gen. 48 Jacob laid hands on Joseph's children and blessed them. Mark 10:16 Jesus laid hands on children and blessed them.

6) For healing.

We see some examples of the laying on of hands for a blessing in the Old Testament of the Bible. In the Old Testament, Jacob blessed Joseph's children in Genesis 48. But it really sprang forth like a river in the New Testament with the ministry of Jesus. That is Who we strive to be like. We have the same Spirit in us as Jesus. We are to be like Jesus. He laid hands on the sick - they were healed. We should do the same.

In Matthew 8:1-3 Jesus cleansed a leper. *Verse 3 " He stretched out His hand and touched him..."* Immediately his leprosy was cleansed.

We also should be speaking to mountains (situations, sickness, problems) to go. In Matthew 8:5-13 Jesus healed the centurion's servant. The centurion said in vs. 8 "just say the word and my servant will be healed." We sometimes speak, we sometimes lay hands on the sick, we sometimes do both.

Matthew 9:18-25 The synagogue official's daughter. She was dead. In vs. 15 Jesus laid hands on her and she arose.

Matthew 9:27-29 Two blind men. In vs 29 Jesus touched their eyes...their eyes were opened.

And with all this there is something of greater importance. Jesus still had compassion on them because they still needed salvation - they were like sheep without a shepherd. So He was a

Shepherd to those who followed Him. He trained and commissioned the disciples to be shepherds to the people.

In. Matthew 10:7-8 He had sent the disciples out and gave them this charge. "And as you go, preach saying, 'The kingdom of heaven is at hand. Heal the sick, raise the dead, cleanse the lepers, cast out demons; Freely you received, freely give.'"

We have the same charge, so begin using your hands.

Why do you think the people brought the children to Jesus? *Mark 10:16 "And He took them in His arms and began blessing them, laying His hands on them."* Also see Mark 10:13-16.

Also in Mark 7:32-35 with the deaf and dumb person. "He took him...put His finger into his ears, and after spitting, He touched his tongue with the saliva," then his ears opened and he spoke plainly. And in Mark 8:22 with the blind man. *vs 23 "... After spitting on his eyes, and laying hands upon him, He asked him; 'Do you see anything?'* His sight was not clear at first so in *vs. 25 Jesus "laid his hands upon his eyes (again) and he began to see everything clearly."*

Great miracles come through the laying on of hands in Jesus' name - so get busy using your hands. We have laid hands on and prayed over horses, cats, other animals and people and have seen them healed physically and emotionally. Sometimes I lay my hand on a person's heart or mind and say, "Peace be with you" and instruct them to say, "I receive it." and they do. Broken, hurt and wounded hearts are healed and confusion in the mind goes - clear thinking is restored.

Also in the Book of Acts 8 the baptism in the Holy Ghost (Holy Spirit) came upon the people through the laying on of hands. We still do this and see the same result.

Hands are laid on people to send them out to minister as we see in Acts 13:2-3.

I Tim. 4:14 mentions that spiritual gifts were bestowed on people "through prophetic utterance with the laying on of hands."

We laid hands on one lady, spoke to her body to be healed, and God healed her instantly of spinalbifada, scoliosis and arthritis. In just a few weeks she became the children's Sunday school teacher at Texas Cowboy Church.

We have also seen God heal backs, necks, arms, headaches and take fever away from many people as we have laid hands on them. One lady at a rodeo school came to the Cowboy Church service and was healed of M.S. (multiple sclerosis). She was running up and down the bleachers on her own power, when earlier she had to be helped to be seated.

I have spoken healing over bull riders and bareback riders with knee injuries at rodeos and watched them ride with no pain after laying hands on them and praying or speaking to the body to line up with the Word of God.

THE GREATEST MIRACLE! - All this is great, but still the greatest miracle is to be born again - to have your sins forgiven and washed away. This is a spiritual miracle. This comes through confession of sin and receiving Jesus as Savior because of His going to the cross to save us and making the way for us to go to heaven and have eternal life. If this is what you want pray this. "Dear God I confess I am a sinner, I need a Savior. I receive Jesus as my Savior and the Lord, the Boss of my life. Thank you for dying on the cross and shedding your Blood to wash away my sins. Right now I am saved; I am a child of God, on my way to heaven. I thank you for making the way for me to go to Heaven. Jesus is now my Lord. In Jesus name I pray - Amen.

Now read the Bible everyday, pray daily, get baptized, meet with other believers often. (Romans 3:10, 3:23, 5:8-9, 6:23, 10:9-10, John 3:16 and be filled with the Holy Spirit. Acts 1:8, Luke 11:13.)

chapter

28

Triumphs Of Faith
Hebrews 11-12:3
(New American Standard Bible)

(1) Now faith is the assurance of things hoped for, the conviction (evidence in NKJ) of things not seen. (2) For by it the men of old gained approval. (3) By faith we understand that the worlds were prepared by the word of God, so that what is seen was not made out of things which are visible. (4) By faith Abel offered to God a better sacrifice than Cain, through which he obtained the testimony that he was righteous, God testifying about his gifts, and through faith, though he is dead, he still speaks. (5) By faith Enoch was taken up so that he would not see death; AND HE WAS NOT FOUND BECAUSE GOD TOOK HIM UP; for he obtained the witness that before his being taken up he was pleasing to God. (6) And without faith it is impossible to please Him, for he who comes to God must believe that He is and that He is a rewarder of those who seek Him. (7) By faith Noah, being warned by God about things not yet seen, in reverence prepared an ark for the salvation of his household, by which he condemned the world, and became an heir of the righteousness which is according to faith. (8) By faith Abraham, when he was called, obeyed by going out to a place which he was to receive for an inheritance; and he went out, not knowing where he was going. (9) By faith he lived as an alien in the land of promise, as in a foreign land, dwelling in tents with Isaac and Jacob, fellow heirs of the same promise; (10) for he was looking for the city which has foundations, whose architect and builder is God. (11) By faith even Sarah herself received ability to conceive, even beyond the proper time of life, since she considered Him faithful who had promised. (12) Therefore there was born even of one man, and him as good as dead at that, as many descendants AS THE STARS OF HEAVEN IN NUMBER, AND INNUMERABLE AS THE SAND WHICH IS BY THE SEASHORE.

(13) All these died in faith, without receiving the promises, but having seen them and having welcomed them from a distance, and having confessed that they were strangers and exiles on the earth. (14) For those who say such things make it clear that they are seeking a country of their own. (15) And indeed if they had been thinking of that country from which they went out, they would have had opportunity to return. (16) But as it is, they desire a better country, that is, a heavenly one. Therefore God is not ashamed to be called their God; for He has prepared a city for them. (17) By faith Abraham, when he was tested, offered up Isaac, and he who had received the promises was offering up his only begotten son; (18) it was he to whom it was said, "IN ISAAC YOUR DESCENDANTS SHALL BE CALLED." (19) He considered that God is able to raise people even from the dead, from which he also received him back as a type. (20) By faith Isaac blessed Jacob and Esau, even regarding things to come. (21) By faith Jacob, as he was dying, blessed each of the sons of Joseph, and worshiped, leaning on the top of his staff. (22) By faith Joseph, when he was dying, made mention of the exodus of the sons of Israel, and gave orders concerning his bones. (23) By faith Moses, when he was born, was hidden for three months by his parents, because they saw he was a beautiful child; and they were not afraid of the king's edict. (24) By faith Moses, when he had grown up, refused to be called the son of Pharaoh's daughter, (25) choosing rather to endure ill-treatment with the people of God than to enjoy the passing pleasures of sin, (26) considering the reproach of Christ greater riches than the treasures of Egypt; for he was looking to the reward. (27) By faith he left Egypt, not fearing the wrath of the king; for he endured, as seeing Him who is unseen. (28) By faith he kept the Passover and the sprinkling of the blood, so that he who destroyed the firstborn would not touch them. (29) By faith they passed through the Red Sea as though they were passing through dry land; and the Egyptians, when they attempted it, were

drowned. (30) By faith the walls of Jericho fell down after they had been encircled for seven days. (31) By faith Rahab the harlot did not perish along with those who were disobedient, after she had welcomed the spies in peace. (32) And what more shall I say? For time will fail me if I tell of Gideon, Barak, Samson, Jephthah, of David and Samuel and the prophets, (33) who by faith conquered kingdoms, performed acts of righteousness, obtained promises, shut the mouths of lions, (34) quenched the power of fire, escaped the edge of the sword, from weakness were made strong, became mighty in war, put foreign armies to flight. (35) Women received back their dead by resurrection; and others were tortured, not accepting their release, so that they might obtain a better resurrection; (36) and others experienced mockings and scourgings, yes, also chains and imprisonment. (37) They were stoned, they were sawn in two, they were tempted, they were put to death with the sword; they went about in sheepskins, in goatskins, being destitute, afflicted, ill-treated (38) (men of whom the world was not worthy), wandering in deserts and mountains and caves and holes in the ground. (39) And all these, having gained approval through their faith, did not receive what was promised, (40) because God had provided something better for us, so that apart from us they would not be made perfect.

Note: You will find the above examples of winning by faith in the Old Testament. Search them out, read the whole story of each. It will build your faith. Remember faith is assurance; faith is evidence that you believe for something and already know it will come into being before you actually see it, hear it, feel it, taste it or touch it. By your faith in God it is a fact already, then it will happen.

Hebrews 12
Jesus, the Example

(1) "Therefore, since we have so great a cloud of witnesses surrounding us, let us also lay aside every encumbrance and the sin which so easily entangles us, and let us run with endurance the race that is set before us, (2) fixing our eyes on Jesus, the author and perfecter of faith, who for the joy set before Him endured the cross, despising the shame, and has sat down at the right hand of the throne of God. (3) For consider Him who has endured such hostility by sinners against Himself, so that you will not grow weary and lose heart."

chapter

29   What Is A Christian?

Acts 11:26 "...And it came about that for an entire year they met with the church, and taught considerable numbers; and the disciples were first called Christians in Antioch."

Paul and Barnabas spent an entire year teaching the new believers in Jesus Christ. When people saw the outcome they called them Christians.

Who is a Christian?

Why were they called Christians?

Why would someone want to be a Christian?

Are Christians really any different than others?

What is a Christian?

First off, the disciples were taught for a year, so they were teachable.

Second, Acts 11:26 said, the "disciples" were called Christians. A disciple is a follower of Christ. It means Christ like. It comes from the word discipline. A Christian leads a disciplined life.

Paul, in 1 Cor. 9:25, talks of "self-control." He continues in verse 26 *"Therefore I run in such a way, as not without aim; I box in such a way, as not beating the air; (27) but I buffet my body and make it my slave, lest possibly, after I have preached to others, I myself should be disqualified."*

Here's more on discipline. *Romans 6:11 "Even so consider yourselves to be dead to sin, but alive to God in Christ Jesus."* and *verse (14) For sin shall not be master over you,..."*

The first place to begin to be a disciple is to repent. Jesus said, *"repent and believe in the gospel."* (Mark 1:15)

Paul told them, (in Acts 2:36) *"that God has made HIm both*

Lord and Christ - this Jesus whom you crucified (37) Now when they heard this, they were pierced to the heart, and said to Peter and the rest of the apostles, 'Brethren, what shall we do?' (38) And Peter said to them, 'Repent, and let each of you be baptized in the name of Jesus Christ for the forgiveness of your sins; and you shall receive the gift of the Holy Spirit.'" Repent means to change your mind, your heart, your direction.

• A Christian is someone who has received Jesus as Savior and Lord and has changed his lifestyle.

• A Christian is someone who understands he needs a Savior. He knows sin separates a person from God and takes them to hell. The Savior brings them out of hell and gives them eternal life in heaven.

• A Christian Walks in love, joy and peace.

• A Christian forgives and does not walk in bitterness and hate.

• A Christian is not ashamed of the gospel (Romans 1:16)

• A Christian understands the power in the name of Jesus. *Acts 3:1-5 "When Peter and John saw the beggar, a man who had been lame all his life, sitting at the gate of the temple, Peter said, 'I do not possess silver and gold, but what I do have I give to you: In the name of Jesus Christ the Nazarene - walk!'"* Vs 7-8 reports that *"immediately his feet and his ankles were strengthened (8) And with a leap, he stood upright and began to walk..."*

• A Christian has authority over the devil, the demons, evil spirits and sin, sickness, disease, distress and troubles. Luke 10:17-19; Mark 16:17-20, John 14:12; John 16:33.

• A Christian has troubles but he has a Deliverer to bring him through to victory. (see John 16:33)

• A Christian shuns evil and the appearance of evil - and moves toward holiness. We are told to "be holy yourselves also in all your behavior." (1 Peter 1:15)

• A Christian is led by the Holy Spirit and not by the flesh. Rom. 8:6; Rom. 8:14; Gal. 5:16-17

• A Christian has "the fruit of the Spirit is love, joy, peace, patience, kindness, goodness, faithfulness, gentleness, self-control..." Gal. 5:22-23

• A Christian helps others.

• A Christian loves God and loves his neighbor. Mark 12:28-31

• A Christian comes out from among sinners and is separate. He honors his holy temple, his body. II *Cor. 6:16 "...For we are the temple of the living God;... (vs 17) 'Therefore come out from their midst and be separate,' says the Lord. 'And do not touch what is unclean; and I will welcome you. (18) And I will be a Father to you, and you shall be sons and daughters to Me,' says the Lord Almighty."*

• A Christian is different than the world.

A person who comes to Christ Jesus comes one way - receives Jesus as Savior - and leaves another way. Zaccheus, a tax-collector, went from greed to generosity.

I Cor. 6:9-11 "Or do you not know that the unrighteous shall not inherit the kingdom of God? Do not be deceived; neither fornicators, nor idolaters, nor adulterers, nor effeminate, nor homosexuals, (10) nor thieves, nor covetous, nor drunkards, nor revilers, nor swindlers, shall inherit the kingdom of God. (11) And such were some of you; but you were washed, but you were sanctified, but you were justified in the name of the Lord Jesus Christ, and in the Spirit of our God." Notice it states they were in one condition but they were washed clean by the blood of Jesus and sanctified or set apart. to do the will of God."

• A Christian follows Christ in water baptism, reads the Bible, and prays often.

• A Christian can ask Jesus to baptize him in the Holy Ghost for power to live an overcoming life.

• A Christian tells others about Jesus.

• A Christian knows Jesus, therefore he knows the Father. (John

14:7)

• A Christian has eternal life. (John 3:36)

Are you tired of not being connected to God? Are you tired of doing things your own way? Are you tired of sin? Are you ready for a change? Are you ready for the Savior?

Do you want eternal life? Do you want to become a Christian - a disciple of Jesus Christ? *Romans 10:13 states "for 'Whoever will call upon the Name of the Lord will be saved.'"* Call on him now. Say, "Dear God I am a sinner. I need a Savior. Forgive my sins. I call to you and receive Jesus Christ as my Savior and Lord. I believe Jesus is the Son of God, that He died on the cross for me and rose again on the third day. I confess right now that Jesus is my Lord. Heaven is my home. I can call God my Father. Holy Spirit help me to live a life pleasing to my Father in heaven. In Jesus name. Amen."

Now get baptized, read the Bible and pray daily, get into a church where you can grow in Christ. (Read Romans 3:10; 3:23, 5:8-9, 6:23, 10:9-10-13, John 3:16, Acts 2:38, Luke 11:13.

Now go live a life pleasing to God. Let your light shine before men and glorify God. You are a Christian. Be different. Be a disciple. Others will see your life and they will call you a Christian.

chapter

30

What's Blocking Your Blessings???

Deuteronomy 11:26-28 "Behold, I set before you this day a blessing and a curse; (27) A blessing, if you obey the commandments of the Lord your God, which I command you this day: (28) And a curse, if you will not obey the commandments of the Lord your God, ..."

God's desire is to bless His people. There are many promises in the Bible to His children concerning blessings. With every promise, there is a condition. Receiving Jesus as Savior and Lord is a free gift and we get heaven in the deal. But, what we do, or don't do, blocks our blessings. We must do our part and walk in God's ways if we are to receive the blessings He has for us. Certain things we do cause us to live under a self-imposed curse. **Let's look at some things that block our blessings** (or turn it around and see what brings our blessings).

(1) Not being a doer of the Word - See *Deut. 11:27 above. Also James 1:22 "But be ye doers of the Word, and not hearers only, deceiving your ownselves."*

(2) Lack of Knowledge - Hosea 4:6 Read the Bible daily - find out what God would have you know and do; sit under good Bible teachers.

(3) Not tithing - 10% of your increase goes to God and His work on the earth. Worship God with your tithes. He will bless you. *Malachi 10 "says to bring your tithes to the storehouse and He will open heaven's windows and pour a blessing on you."* This is the Bible pattern established before the Law when Abraham tithed. We tithe to Jesus by giving to the apostles, prophets, evangelists, pastors and teachers.

(4) Lack of repentance - *Prov. 1:23 "Turn you at my reproof, behold I will pour out My Spirit unto you, I will make* *known My words to you." Luke 13:3 "...unless you repent, you will all likewise perish."*

(5) Conforming to the world's standards instead of God's - Romans 12:2 *"And do not be conformed to the world, but be transformed by the renewing of your mind, that you may prove what the will of God is, that which is good and acceptable and perfect."*

(6) Failing to get into the presence of God - We need to pray everyday and throughout the day. Get into God's presence. Get His direction-See Luke 18:1 and Matthew 7:7.

(7) Walking in Unforgiveness - The Bible says if you don't forgive others - God won't forgive you. Choose to forgive, even if you don't feel like doing so, your feeling will catch up later. See Mark 11:25-26.

(8) Quenching the Spirit - Do not put out or turn off the work of the Holy Spirit in your life. He is the Comforter, your Teacher and Helper. *1 Thess. 5:19 "Do not quench the Spirit;"*

(9) Not being a good steward - (caretaker) of the gifts, talents and abilities God has given you) *Luke 19:26 "...I tell you, that to everyone who has shall more be given, but from the one who does not have, even what he has shall be taken away."* USE IT OR LOSE IT!

(10) Slothfulness - (not being a good worker) Prov. 10:4 He becomes poor that deals with a slack hand: but the hand of the diligent makes rich.

(11) Not guarding your mouth - *Proverbs 6:2 "Thou art snared with the words of your mouth..."* Be careful what you say. *Proverbs 8:21 "Death and life are in the power of the tongue and those who love it will eat its fruit."*

(12) Not guarding your heart - *Proverbs 4:23 "Keep thy heart with all diligence; for out of it are the issues of life."*

(13) Unconfessed Sin - If you have sin, confess it, get forgiven of it, learn from it and move on to do better. 1 John 1:9.

(14) Not being a giver - *Luke 6:38 "Give and it shall be given unto you..."* God loves a cheerful giver. 1 Cor. 9:7.

(15) Not making Jesus Lord over every area of you life - Make Jesus Lord over your job, your money, your dress, your thoughts, your family, your desires - He is Lord of all. *Phil 2:11 "and that every tongue should confess that Jesus Christ is Lord, to the glory of God the Father."*

(16) Not knowing Jesus - and receiving Him as Savior and Lord. This one will block your greatest blessing of all - going to Heaven and having eternal life. If you have not received Jesus pray with sincerity.

"Lord forgive me of my sins, I receive Jesus into my heart, into my life right now as Savior and Lord. Thank you for dying for me and shedding your blood to wash away my sins. Thank you for making a home in heaven for me and giving me eternal life. Holy Spirit guide me and help me to be the child of God You want me to be." In Jesus name I pray. Amen. *John 3:36 "He who believes in the Son (Jesus) has eternal life; but he who does not obey the Son shall not see life, but the wrath of God abides on him."*

Things that bring Blessings! Turn the above things around and do them and the sure blessings of God will flow in your life. Be a doer of the Word, CHOOSE BLESSINGS! EXPECT BLESS-INGS! EXPERIENCE BLESSINGS!

chapter
31

Which Voice Pleases You?
God's, The Devil's, Other People or Self

Isaiah 30:21 "Your ears shall hear a word behind you, saying, 'This is the way, walk in it,' whenever you turn to the right hand or whenever you turn to the left."

There are a lot of voices in the world. Opinions are abundant. What we need in making the right decisions is God's opinion. Learn to discern the voice of God. He will never contradict His Word, the Bible. When you sit under Bible teachers or preachers or listen to other people, **always** check them out in the Word. Obey God's word by faith and you will win in life.

The Voice of God - *Genesis 2:16-17 "And the Lord commanded man saying, "Of every tree of the garden you may freely eat; (17) but of the tree of the knowledge of good and evil you shall not eat, for in the day that you eat of it you shall surely die."*

The Voice of the Devil - *Genesis 3:4 "Then the serpent said to the woman (Eve), 'You will not surely die.'"* So in verse 6 she took of the fruit of the tree and gave some to her husband, Adam, to eat. At this point, sin entered into the world. The Lord gave them life, but they chose death through Eve being deceived and Adam's disobedience. God also had planted "the tree of life" in the middle of the garden. They could have chosen to eat of that tree and lived forever. (see vs22)

The Voice of Others - Adam listened to his wife instead of God. *Genesis 3:17-19 (17) "Then to Adam, He (God) said, 'Because you have heeded the voice of your wife, and have eaten from the tree of which I commanded you, saying, 'You shall not eat of it; Cursed is the ground for you sake; In toil you shall eat of it all the days of your life.'" (18) Both thorns and thistles it shall grow for* you; and you will eat the plants of the field; (19) "In the sweat of your face you shall eat bread, till you return to the ground, for out of it you were taken; For dust you are, and to dust you shall return." God's desire for them was life but now they sinned and experienced spiritual death, which is separation from God. Physical death set in, and their bodies would someday die.

The Voice of their own self-the flesh - What brought this about? The wrong voice pleased them. When they heard the voice of the devil, when Adam listened to someone's voice that contradicted God's, then their voice chimed in - t**he voice of their own flesh**. Genesis 3:6 shows that it pleased Eve's flesh so she took it.

Always go with the voice of God over the voice of the devil, your spouse, your friends, your kin, your boss, your co-workers, your church, any other group, or your own voice that wants to please the flesh more than God.

Romans 8:6 "For the mind set on the flesh is death, but the mind set on the Spirit is life and peace." and *verse 8 says "and those who are in the flesh cannot please God."*

Which voice pleases you? **Often,** the voice of the devil and the voice of people will please your flesh - so that is the voice you listen to and go after. It is the voice of the Holy Spirit that produces life and blessings. *Romans 8:14 "For all who are being led by the Spirit of God, these are the sons of God."*

Obedience brings blessings. Rebellion brings curses. See *Isaiah 1:19-20 "If you are willing and obedient, you shall eat the good of the land' (20) but if your refuse and rebel you shall be devoured by the sword; For the mouth of the Lord has spoken."*

Saul listened to Jesus, in Acts 9:4-6, when He appeared to him on the road to Damascus as he was going out to persecute Christians. Jesus said, "'Saul, Saul, why are you persecuting Me?' Saul said, 'Who are Thou Lord?' He said, 'I am Jesus whom you are persecuting, but rise, and enter the city, and it shall be told you what you must do.'" The Result - Saul received Jesus as His Savior, was baptized in water, was baptized in the Holy Spirit, became a mighty man of God and wrote most of the New Testament books of the Bible. Before he had been listening to his religious teachers, his fellow men, his own voice and was prompted by the devil. Now, Saul (later known as Paul, the apostle) not only heard the voice of God but did what he was told and thousands upon thousands of lives have been changed by his work for the Lord.

Jesus also had a choice when He was tempted by the devil in the desert. (See Matthew 4:1-11) In the first temptation, the voice of the devil tempted Jesus to change the stones into bread; this would please the flesh, especially after 40 days of fasting - but Jesus desired to please the Father in Heaven more than His own flesh. He overcame the temptation and showed us how to overcome temptations to sin. Always seek God's will first, speak the Word, and do what the Father says to do. Listen to His voice and do what He says.

In the Garden, just before Jesus died for our sins, His own voice uttered these words *Luke 22:42 "...Father, if Thou art willing, remove this cup from me;" (but He quickly added this) "yet not My will, but Thine be done."* Pleasing His Father was too important to Him to not go to the cross to die. Making a way for forgiveness of sin so me and you could go to Heaven was too important to Jesus to not go to the cross. **No matter what any voice said, Jesus chose God's voice** - and for this we can have eternal life and abundant life here on earth.

John 10:27 Jesus said, "My sheep hear My voice, and I know them, and they follow Me; (28) and I give eternal life to them, and they shall never perish; and no one shall snatch them out of the Father's hand."

The voice of God says, "receive Jesus, receive eternal life, receive blessings."

1.) Receive Jesus by faith.

2.) Many voices will tell you how to get to heaven. Listen

to God's voice as you read the Bible and hear the voice of the Holy Spirit. Jesus is the only way to heaven.

3.) Repent - change directions. Do what God says to do.

4.) By faith - Receive Jesus as Savior and Lord today and enjoy the benefits of eternal life and heaven. Win Forever!!!

5.) *Ephes. 2:8-9, 10 (8) For by grace you have been saved through faith; and that not of yourselves, it is the gift of God; (9) not as a result of works, so that no one may boast. (10) For we are His workmanship, created in Christ Jesus for good works, which God prepared beforehand so that we would walk in them.*

John 3:36 "He who believes in the Son has eternal life; but he who does not obey the Son will not see life, but the wrath of God abides on him."

John 14:6 Jesus said to him, "I am the way, and the truth, and the life; no one comes to the Father but through Me.

Romans 10:9-10, 13 that if you confess with your mouth Jesus as Lord, and believe in your heart that God raised Him from the dead, you will be saved; (10) for with the heart man believes, resulting in righteousness, and with the mouth he confesses, resulting in salvation. (13) for "WHOEVER WILL CALL ON THE NAME OF THE LORD WILL BE SAVED."

Listen to God's Voice - do what He says and expect blessings!

chapter

32

Why Read The Bible?

COWBOY BIBLE

NEW AMERICAN STANDARD
NEW TESTAMENT

Christian Cowboys
and Friends

Jesus is Lord!

One Word From God
Can Change Your Life
Forever

John 6:63 (Jesus said) "It is the Spirit who gives life; the flesh profits nothing; the words that I speak are spirit and life."

Isaiah 55:11 "So shall My word be that goes forth from My mouth; it shall not return to Me void, but it shall accomplish that which I please, and it shall prosper in the thing for which I sent it."

When we say, "one word from God can change your life, that can mean one word, one Scripture verse, one thought from a group of verses together, one idea, one correction, one direction or one instruction, etc.

The Roman centurion (officer in the army) who came to Jesus, in Matthew 8:5-13, understood authority and power of words when spoken by those in authority. When he told Jesus that his servant was sick at home, Jesus offered to go to him and heal him. In verse 8, the centurion knew Jesus did not have to physically go there, and he said in part, "just say the word and my servant will be healed." The result in vs. 13 "the servant was healed that very hour."

We desperately need to understand the power of the Word of God, and how it can change our lives. Multitudes of people came to Jesus, and still do, to be saved form hell, to be healed of

111

sicknesses, to get peace of mind, to get their priorities in line with God's will, to be set free from all types of bondages, addictions and bad attitudes. Yes, they came one way and left another - better than when they came. Often His word was short, like- "Be healed." or "Come, follow me" or "Your faith has saved you" or even when He spoke to the wind, "Peace, be still." Other times, He spent hours and even days giving instruction.

If you have an area of need, go to God, go to His Word, the Bible, and get a word from Him. Our own thought and ideas fall short; the gospel will show us everything we need to know to walk in victory in this life, and even right on into eternity.

Since the answers for life and for eternity are in the Bible we need to be well acquainted, well equipped with the Word of God. What goes in you will come out of you - in your thoughts and in your actions.

If you have a need right now for direction, correction, instruction, healing, salvation or whatever go to God's Word and get a promise for yourself and your situation. Ask God for a rhema (rayma) word. A rhema, is a word from God, spoken into your spirit and into your heart. As you read the Bible, it's like a particular scripture, or a story in the Bible will jump out of the pages and go right inside of you. It's a rhema! It is more real than what you see, feel, taste, touch or hear. As you quote, speak and believe the Word, your faith will be built up and you will see circumstances, people and situations change.

The word affects you spiritually, physically, mentally, emotionally, socially and financially. It affects your family, your direction and your very life in every area. It's too important to neglect. You must read the Word, hear the Word, pray the Word and speak the Word.

Now let's look at a few of God's promises in the different areas.

SPIRITUALLY - ETERNAL LIFE - *John 3:16 "For God so loved the* world that He gave His only begotten Son that whoever believes in Him should not perish, but have eternal life." (Also Mark 16:15, John 3:36, Romans 10:9-10, 13, I John 5:10-13).

PHYSICALLY - HEALING - *Matthew 8:16-17 "And when evening had come, they brought to Him many who were demon - possessed; and He cast out the spirits with a word, and healed all who were ill. (17) in order that what was spoken through Isaiah the prophet might be fulfilled, saying, 'HE HIMSELF TOOK OUR INFIRMITIES, AND CARRIED AWAY OUR DISEASES.'"* (Also see Mark 16:18, I Peter 1:24).

PHYSICALLY - SOUNDNESS - *Prov. 4:20-22 "My Son, give attention to my words; Incline your ear to my sayings. (21) Do not let them depart from your eyes; Keep them in the midst of your heart; (22) For they are life to those who find them, And health to all their flesh."* (Also III John 2)

MENTALLY - *I Corinthians 2:16 "For WHO HAS KNOWN THE MIND OF THE LORD, THAT HE SHOULD INSTRUCT HIM? But we have the mind of Christ."* (Also see Mark 5:15).

EMOTIONALLY - Jesus said in *John 14:27 "Peace I leave with you; My peace I give to you; not as the world gives, do I give to you. Let not your heart be troubled not let it be fearful."*

SOCIALLY - *Ephesians 4:32 "And be kind to one another, tenderhearted, forgiving each other, just as God in Christ also has forgiven you."* (Also Mark 5:19) See Luke 5:13 the cleansed leper could go back to society and friends.

FINANCES - *Philippians 4:19 "And my God shall supply all your needs according to His riches in glory in Christ Jesus."* (Remember this is a promise to those who are givers into the ministry). (Also II Cor. 9:8, Ephes. 4:28, Mark 10:29-30, Malachi 3:10-11).

FAMILY - Everyday life: *Colossians 3:18-21 "Wives, be subject to your husbands, as is fitting in the Lord. (19) Husbands, love your wives, and do not be embittered against them. (20) Children, be obedient to your parents in all things, for this is well-pleasing to the*

Lord. (21) *Fathers, do not exasperate your children, that they may not lose heart."*

DIRECTION - *Proverbs 3:6 "In all your ways acknowledge Him (God) and He will direct your paths."* (Also see James 1:5).

YOUR VERY LIFE - *Psalms 32:8 "I will instruct you and teach you in the way you should go, I will guide you with my eye,"* James 1:5 - God will give you wisdom when you ask for it.

Remember, the Word of God is powerful. Jesus said we are to speak to our mountains and whatever we say will be done. Be sure to speak the Word and watch your mountains be removed.

As you continue to read the Word you will definitely change. You will think differently and act differently.

Psalm 119:105 "Your word is a lamp to my feet and a light to my path." Let God's word continue to guide, correct, instruct, change you and the things in your life, and to confirm God's will for you. Do not go on without it - ever. We need it too much. Praise God.

Where to start? Start with the spiritual first. Get your heart right with God. The Word says in *Romans 10:13 "Whoever calls on the name of the Lord will be saved?"* If you never have done this let's do it now. Pray this: "Lord, I am calling on you now. I am lost and I want to be saved. Save me now. Forgive all my sins. I receive what Jesus did for me on the cross when he died for my sins. I receive Jesus now as my Savior and Lord. Thank you for the Word of God. Thank You for eternal life. Holy Spirit teach me the Word so I can live the life God wants me to. In Jesus name - Amen. Now say, "Praise God, I am saved." His word instructs you to now read the Bible daily, pray daily, get baptized, meet often with other believers and to grow in Christ.

chapter

33

What You "Believe" Determines Your Destiny

Mark 11:24 "Therefore I say to you, all things for which you pray and ask, believe that you have received them, and they shall be granted to you."

What you believe, <u>truly believe</u>, with all your heart, settles your destiny for eternity and for your days on this earth. (See John 3:16, John 3:36, John 10:10, Romans 10:9-10, Acts 27:25).

You have heard it said, "You have what you say", but remember "you say what you believe" so you really get what you believe for. Out of the abundance of the heart, the mouth speaks. What you believe is so very important. You will act on what you believe.

Caleb and Joshua believed God, (Num. 14:8-9), and were ready to take the land from the giants living there because God said they could go in and possess it. But the other ten spies believed what the circumstances looked like. Those ten turned all Israel against the plan of God. So those 20 years of age and older never entered the promise land, except for Caleb and Joshua. The ten said that the giants were too strong and would defeat Israel.

115

Caleb and Joshua said, "we are able to take the land" and they eventually went in to take it. The rest got what they believed. *Numbers 14:2 "Say to them, 'As I live,' says the Lord, just as you have spoken in My hearing, so I will do to you.'"* The ten died of the plague by the Lord. They spoke what they believed - it became their destiny.

The Lesson? - Always believe God!

Abraham believed God, in *Genesis 15:6 "And he believed in the Lord, and He accounted it to him for righteousness."* Abraham, at 75 years old, was childless, but God promised him an heir and a multitude of descendants. He believed God. At that moment God saw him as righteous. Righteous is to be in right standing with God. The moment you believe God, you are righteous in His eyes. Abraham had to keep believing, in "hope against hope." His promise of a son came 25 years later. When he was 100 years old, his son, Isaac, was born. His wife was 90.

From the time you believe God for a good report, a promise, a dream or vision to come to pass - you will have many opportunities, many challenges to stop believing. Don't stop - keep believing. God is faithful. It may look impossible but not with God. *Matthew 10:2 "Looking upon them, Jesus said, 'With men it is impossible but not with God; for all things are possible with God.'"*

What you believe is important. You will act on what you believe.

The Roman Centurion had great faith concerning the healing of his servant by Jesus (See story - Matt. 8:5-13) *Verse 13 "And Jesus said to the centurion, 'Go your way, let it be done to you as you have believed.' And the servant was healed that very hour."*

The father of the demon possessed son brought his son to the disciples; they did not totally believe, but Jesus did. Look at what He said, *Mark 9:23 "And Jesus said to him; 'If you can! All things are possible to him who believes.'" (vs 24) "Immediately the boy's father cried out and began saying, 'I do believe; help my unbelief.'"* Then Jesus cast out the deaf and dumb spirit.

Jesus scolded His disciples for their unbelief. Jesus spoke well of those who did believe. Which one are you? "Believing" prayers change the world.

Believe Things Will Work Out "Exactly" Like God Says They Will

Also, be like Paul, and believe God that it will turn out "exactly" like God says it will. Paul was in a ship on his way to Rome to testify before Caesar. The ship was in a storm; an angel of God told Paul their lives would be spared. The soldiers listened to Paul's instructions and 276 people made it to the shore alive after the ship had wrecked, because Paul said this, in Acts 27:25, "Therefore, keep you your courage, men, for I believe God, that it will turn out exactly as I have been told." Don't stop believing when you get a partial blessing. Thank God for every blessing along the way, but keep believing for the full blessing. Keep believing until it turns out "exactly" like God says it will. If you are believing for healing and get some relief, don't just say "Thank you Lord," and quit believing for the total healing and good health. Keep believing for the full promise of total good health. If you are believing to be debt free and you get a financial blessing that helps a lot and you get some relief, thank God; don't stop there - keep believing for the rest to come until it turns out exactly like you began believing God for it to. (III John 2)

Doubt and do without -or- Believe and receive

What you believe will change your destiny, your finances, your health, your family, your success in this life on earth and eternity.

When Jesus raised Lazarus from the dead, some believed in Jesus, but some went away. Which one are you?

There are believers in the gospel of Jesus and non-believers. This is the way it will turn out.

Mark 16:15-16 "And He said to them, 'Go into all the

117

world and preach the gospel (the good news that Jesus saves) to all creation. (16) He who has believed and has been baptized shall be saved; but he who has disbelieved shall be condemned.'"

What do you believe in your heart? It's important.

Romans 10:9-11, 13 "that if you confess with your mouth Jesus as Lord, and believe in your heart that God raised Him from the dead, you shall be saved; (10) for with the heart man believes, resulting in righteousness, and with the mouth he confesses, resulting in salvation. (11) For the Scripture says, 'Whoever believes in Him will not be disappointed.'" (13) for 'Whoever will call upon the name of the Lord will be saved.'"

Pray What You Believe: Are you a sinner lost without God? Do you believe Jesus is the Savior who died for your sins so you can have eternal life. If so pray this: Dear God I am a sinner. I need a Savior. I believe that Jesus Christ is the Son of God, I believe He is the Savior, He is the way to Heaven. I ask you to forgive me and I receive Jesus now into my heart and life to be my Savior and the Lord, the Boss of my life. Thank you for eternal life. I believe you will help me live a better life now. In Jesus name. Amen.

chapter

34 Run To Win

I Corinthians 9:24 "Do you not know that those who run in a race all run, but only one receives the prize? Run in such a way that you may win.

There is a way to win in life!

God desires that you win in life. He has designed you to be a winner. A cowboy preacher I know has taught us to say, "I am not a sinner going somewhere to sin; I am a winner going somewhere to win."

Winning takes effort! Champions practice, champions train, champions stay focused on the goal of success, champions are not distracted or deterred from winning, champions put out their best effort. Jesus is a Champion. He looked death in the face and went to the cross because He has the heart of a finisher and a winner. He went to hell to get the captives; He got the keys to death, hell and the grave. He rose again to live forever so we could also. His crown is secure. Because of Him our future is secure. *Romans 8:37 says "...we are more than conquerors through Him who loved us."*

I Cor. 9:25 "And everyone who competes in the games exercises self control in all things. They then do it to receive a perishable wreath, but we an imperishable."

Earthly prizes are nice but our prize in Christ Jesus is eternal - think about it. Determine that *"sin will not be master over me" (Rom 6:14).* If you are not determined to follow Jesus with all your heart you will fall. *Rom 6:18 "and having been freed from sin, you became slaves of righteousness."* The areas you are determined not to sin in are the areas you will be righteous in. There are some areas the devil does not even tempt me in - he knows I won't go for it. There are others areas I am not as strong in and the devil waits for an opportune moment to tempt me into falling into sin. Recently I told the devil, "This is not an opportune moment. I submit to God. I resist you. You must flee." (See James 4:7)

When we do sin, the best thing to do, is repent quickly, get forgiven, get back into obedience - determine not to stay down, not to stay in sin. Determine this - "Thy kingdom come, Thy will will be done in my life." There is worldly sorrow which produces death (because there is no change of heart and lifestyle) and there is godly sorrow which produces repentance. (See II Cor. 7:9-10) Repentance is being sorry enough over your sin to change your heart, your mind and your direction. Without repentance you will perish (Luke 13:3). James 1:22 reminds us to *"be a doer of the Word and not a hearer only deceiving yourselves."* (KJV)

Remember, we are talking about life on earth, and about eternity.

I Cor. 9:26 "Therefore I run in such a way, as not without aim; I box in such a way, as not beating the air."

To win we must have a target, a finish line in mind. We must take aim. Our aim is to do the will of the Father. We will smash the enemy and aim at living a life pleasing to God. *Heb. 12:1-2 tells us, to "lay aside every encumbrance and the sin which so easily entangles us and to run with endurance the race that is set before us (2) fixing our eyes on Jesus, the author and perfector [finisher (KJV) of our faith who for the joy set before Him endured the cross, despising the shame, and has set down at the right hand of the throne of God."* We were the joy set before Him.

I Cor. 9:27 'but I buffet my body and make it a my slave, lest possibly after I have preached to others, I myself should be disqualified."

Determine this - "My flesh will not rule - my spirit will rule. The Spirit of God in me will rule." Col. 3:15 "And let the peace of Christ rule in your hearts,..." Jesus Christ is the ruler.
To win do this:
• I buffet my body. I get in shape.
• I will take time for God.
• I will read the Bible everyday for instruction, direction and correction
• I will pray everyday.
• I will seek first the kingdom of God and His righteousness.
• I will flee from youthful lust.
• I will do that which is right, good and true.
• I will make Jesus my Lord in every area. He is Lord - Adonai - the Master of my life.
• I am filled with the Holy Spirit and have a <u>fresh</u> anointing in my life.
• I walk in love and power of the Holy Spirit.

Jesus is the only way to the Father, the only way to the eternal life, the only way to abundant life and the only way to the life of a winner. Jesus is the "ALL TIME ALL AROUND CHAMPION WINNER IN LIFE". Heb. 4:15 says, He was *"tempted in all things as we are, yet without sin."* He came to die for us and He came to live among us to show us how to live and not sin. He won over sin, sickness, disease, discouragement, death and hell. Jesus is Lord!

<u>Being a winner in life and eternity:</u> Jesus is Lord. To be a winner in this life and for eternity, you must receive Jesus Christ as your Savior and Lord. He died for your sins on the cross to shed His blood to wash you clean. But you must receive Him to be the winner God wants you to be. Pray this. "Oh God, I am a sinner; I ask you to forgive me. I receive Jesus Christ, your Son, as my Savior and I receive what He did for me on the cross. I receive forgiveness of my sins. I make Jesus the Lord, the Boss of my life so I can run in such a way that I will win. Jesus baptize me in the Holy Spirit. Holy Spirit, help me live a life pleasing to my Father in heaven. In Jesus name, Amen." Now read the Bible everyday, pray everyday, get water baptized, ask Jesus to baptize you in the Holy Spirit for power, meet with other believers often. See Romans 3:10, 3:23, 5:8-9, 6:23, 10:9-10, 13; John 3:16, Luke 3:16, Luke 11:13, Acts 1:5, 8, Acts 2:38, Matt. 28:19-20, Heb. 10:24-25.

Now, run by faith with the Lord Jesus, empowered by the Holy Spirit, determined to believe God the Father and His Word.

Reach out to the finish line by faith and win in this life and into eternity.

Faith in Jesus will move your mountains. Speak life and victory to your future by faith.

Trust God and *"Faith It To Win!"*

TRAIL TO HEAVEN

Romans 3:10 - There is none righteous, not even one.

Romans 3:23 - For all have sinned and fall short of the glory of God.

Romans 5:8 - But God demonstrates His own love toward us, in that while we were yet sinners, Christ died for us.

Romans 6:23 - For the wages of sin is death, but the free gift of God is eternal life in Christ Jesus our Lord.

Romans 10:8-10 - (8) But what does it say? The word is near you, in your mouth and in your heart - that is, the word of faith which we are preaching, (9) that if you confess with your mouth Jesus as Lord, and believe in your heart that God raised Him from the dead, you shall be saved; (10) for with the heart man believes, resulting in righteousness, and with the mouth he confesses, resulting in salvation.

Romans 10:13 - for, "Whoever will call on the name of the Lord will be saved." You can know you are saved, your sins are forgiven and you have a home in heaven, eternal life with God forever.

John 3:16 - For God so loved the world, that He gave His only begotten Son, that whoever believes in Him should not perish, but have eternal life.

Revelation 3:20 (Jesus said) "Behold, I stand at the door and knock; if anyone hears My voice and opens the door, I will come into him, and will dine with him, and he with Me. Receive Jesus today by praying a prayer like this:

Dear God, I am sorry for my sins. I ask you to forgive me of all my sins; I turn away from sin and I turn to you. I accept Jesus as my Savior and my Lord right now. Thank you Jesus for dying on the cross and shedding your blood for me to wash my sins away. I confess right now that Jesus, You are my Lord. Thank you for giving me a home in Heaven. Baptize me in the Holy Spirit. Dear Holy Spirit, I ask you to guide me all the days of my life. Thank you God that I can call you my Father and thank you for giving me eternal life. I praise you! In Jesus name, I pray.

Turn to the book of John and read it through.

(1) Get water baptized (2) Ask Jesus to baptize (fill and immerse) you in the Holy Spirit (3) Pray Daily (4) Read the Bible everyday (5) Confess Jesus as Lord to others (6) Meet regularly with other Christians in church and Bible studies (7) Grow in Christ.

To be placed on our mailing list write us at:
CHRISTIAN COWBOYS & FRIENDS
P.O. Box 187, Blanco, Texas 78606 • (830) 386-4936

Faith It To Win!

To be placed on our mailing list write us at:
Christian Cowboys & Friends
P.O. Box 187, Blanco, Texas 78606 • (830) 386-4936

Additional Teaching material by Ronnie Christian

- **Books**
  - Leadership, Followship, Relationship - $6.00 + $1.00 S&H
  - Hang On To Your Hope - $12.00 + $2.00 S&H
  - Miracles Among The Cowboys! - $12.00 + $2.00 S&H
  - Faith It To Win! - $12.00 + $2.00 S&H

We also publish
  - Christian Cowboys and Friends Teaching/Newsletter
    ten to twelve times per year

Suggested gift for this publication is $15.00 per year/$25.00 two years. Add $10.00 per year for Canada and $15.00 per year for other countries. Send "U.S." funds.

To get on mail list send request to Address below.

- **Cowboy Bible** - New American Standard Version with Rodeo artwork on the cover (you will get additional literature with your order) - $9.00
  <u>Notice:</u> Countries out of USA <u>must</u> send $16.00 "U.S. Funds" money order

Consider the above items for yourself or as a gift to a friend, co-workers or family members. Call, write, or e-mail.
Christian Cowboys and Friends
P.O. Box 187, Blanco, TX 78606
(830) 386-4936
Email: rcrodeo@christiancowboy.org
Website: www.christiancowboy.org

<u>Cowboy Partner</u> - Become a Cowboy Partner in this ministry by sending us out with finances and prayers to reach cowboys/cowgirls and others with the Good News of Jesus Christ. Our victory is in Jesus.

ORDER FORM
Great as a gift!

Order Books for family, friends, co-workers and others as a gift and witnessing tool for Jesus.

*Fill out the form below to order books
by Ronnie Christian*

# of books

_____ **Faith It To Win!**
    $12.95 + $2.00 S&H $_____

_____ **Miracles Among The Cowboys!**
    $12.00 + $2.00 S&H $_____

_____ **Hang On To Your Hope**
    $12.00 + $2.00 S&H $_____

_____ **Leadership, Followship, Relationship**
    $6.00 + $1.00 S&H $_____

TOTAL $_____

Order 10 or more and get 25% discount

Send Check or Money Order to:
Christian Cowboys and Friends
P.O. Box 187, Blanco, TX 78606
(830) 386-4936

Name _____

Address _____

State_____ Zip_____

Phone_____ Email_____

125

CPSIA information can be obtained
at www.ICGtesting.com
Printed in the USA
FSOW02n0701040615
7648FS